Sacred Body, Sacred Soul

A Healing Journey Through Shame & Self-Criticism with Radical Self-Love

By Tiffany Cano

For information, permissions, or bulk orders, contact: Tiffany Cano, www.HighlyPerceptivePeopleAcademy.com

ISBN: 979-8-9988507-0-7

Ebook - EPUB: 979-8-9988507-1-4

First edition: June 10, 2025

Cover design by Tiffany Cano

Edited and Formatted by Kristin Campbell

Published by Tiffany Cano

Printed in the United States of America

Author's Note on Collaboration

Parts of this book were lovingly crafted with the support of AI technology, which served as a creative partner in organizing ideas, refining language, and helping bring my vision to life more efficiently.

Every message, story, and teaching was guided with love.

This collaboration reflects the beautiful merging of ancient wisdom with modern tools, reminding us that support comes in many forms when we're open to receiving it.

Love

+

Boundaries

=

Feeling Safe

Dedication

To the brave, radiant women

who chose to rise—

not alone, but in the embrace

of sisterhood, wisdom, and love.

To the ones who faced their shadows,

tended to their wounds,

and remembered their sacredness

through the reflection of other incredible women.

This is for you—

the woman you are now,

the woman you've always been,

and the woman who is still unfolding.

May this book be a mirror,

a healing balm,

and a celebration

of your sacred body

and your luminous soul.

Acknowledgement

With all my heart, I give thanks to God—
my Source, my Beloved, my constant companion.
It is through Divine grace that I have been given the sacred opportunity to love, to serve, and facilitate energy healing.
Every word in this book is a prayer of devotion,
a reflection of my soul's yes to walk this path of light and transformation.
To my Spiritual Teachers, especially Paramahansa Yogananda and Master Choa Kok Sui, and my Mentors—
thank you for your wisdom, presence, and example.
You have held space for my becoming,
seen me through initiations of the heart,
and reminded me again and again
that the sacred is not separate,
but alive within every breath, every body, every soul.
I also want to thank those who hurt, dishonored, or betrayed me along the way. Your actions became unexpected teachers, helping me grow stronger in my boundaries, deeper in compassion, and more devoted to living with love and integrity.
It is an honor to share this offering,
in service to God,
and to the awakening of all who are ready
to   remember   their   Divine   essence.

Table of Contents

Foreword

"As the reigning Mrs. Asia USA, a spiritual healer, and someone devoted to guiding others through transformational healing, I have seen how deeply disconnected many people feel from their own sacredness. Sacred Body, Sacred Soul arrives as a balm for those tender places, offering a path of remembrance, restoration, and radiant self-love.

Tiffany Cano is not only my dear friend and trusted co-facilitator of the Royal Rebirth Retreat, but also a profound lightworker whose intuitive gifts have touched countless lives—including mine. Together, Tiffany and I have had the honor of appearing in the transformational documentaries Pillars of Power and Rise of the Lioness, where the message is clear: true greatness comes from healing, from reclaiming who we really are.

In this book, Tiffany brings the same powerful, heart-centered healing she brings to the retreats and the screen. Sacred Body, Sacred Soul invites you to come home to your sacredness—not through force, but through grace, compassion, and deep honoring. Let it hold you. Let it transform you. Let it help you rise."

— Dr. Angela Kung, Mrs. Asia USA, Spiritual Healer, Featured in Pillars of Power and Rise of the Lioness movies

Happy Endorsements for Sacred Body, Sacred Soul:

"I genuinely love the book, Sacred Body, Sacred Soul! The layout, featuring clear and approachable sections and steps, makes it incredibly easy to read and follow. The personal stories you share are not only remarkable but also deeply relatable. You have created a genuinely safe and enjoyable space for a transformative and personal healing journey, complete with affirmations, exercises, and individual healing practices. Truly remarkable and inspiring! I will definitely turn to this book for my own benefit while also sharing the amazing healing experience with others. I eagerly anticipate the next book in the series!"

~ Angelique Marie

Founder/CEO- Project H.A.L.O. (Hope. Advocate. Learn. Overcome.)

Artist. Author. Advocate.

"Tiffany takes on an authentic, real, and transformational journey into our body. She blends the tools of mind, body, and spirit, and keeps it focussed and practical so you can make those small but massively impactful changes as she shares her expert wisdom, tools, and client stories of inspiration, empowerment, and awakening.

I love how she breaks down the exercises and actions into memorable A-Z steps so it is easily applicable and understandable!

My favourite parts are remembering to live in the now, it's not time to keep waiting, you are enough NOW, as well as examining where our old programming comes from and how to change it! Particularly with hands on the body and communicating directly with it. Simple but sooo effective/powerful We forget just how miraculous we are and that the power to heal is in our hands. Tiffany does a wonderful job of reminding us of this and how to give us our power back with love, healing and trusting.

Be willing to explore and treat yourself to your body soul makeover.

Fabulous Tiffany!"

~ Amanda Steadman, Hypnotherapist & Channeler

AmandaSteadman.com

"Trust. It's the key to our growth and healing, yet one without the other leaves the journey incomplete. In Sacred Body, Sacred Soul, Tiffany Cano offers a path for you to connect with what wants to be exhaled—the old, buried thoughts, feelings, and emotions that invisibly hold you back. You can come home to yourself again, and Tiffany shows you how. I love this book!"

~ Stephanie McAuliffe, Transformation Coach, Healer, Founder of The Way of the Diamond Warrior

"When I started working with Tiffany, I was feeling stuck, disconnected, and overwhelmed. Through her healing work, she helped me to release decades of shame, fear, and emotional pain that I didn't even realize I was carrying. It's like I found myself again, and now I remember my power, my purpose, and my ability to feel joy."

~ Penelope Schmicker, Retired Midwife, Energy Practitioner

"Tiffany is an exceptional mentor and coach. As someone with an engineering mindset, I appreciated how she guided me to explore the science behind energy healing in ways that made perfect sense to me. Through her guidance, I not only transformed how I approach challenges in my career and personal life, but I also experienced compelling, lasting results. Her coaching helped me advance rapidly in my profession while creating more balance and genuine joy across every area of my life."

~ June Kare, Engineering Leader

"This book is a beautiful, powerful reminder that emotional healing is essential for true spiritual growth. Through her words, Tiffany softly guides you to confront our wounds with self love and compassion. She shows how healing our emotions can lead us to a deeper connection with ourselves and our higher power. It's a must-read for anyone on the path to healing inner wounds, seeking peace and striving for spiritual growth."

~ Dr. Lisa Lowe, Founder and President of Silver Management Solutions

"Sacred Body, Sacred Soul is a deeply meaningful and powerful guide for anyone seeking true healing and transformation. Tiffany Cano is a masterful healer who helps you uncover and release the hidden blocks that hold you back from living your best life. If you've ever struggled with shame, self-criticism, or feeling disconnected from your worth, this book is for you. Tiffany offers a compassionate path forward, helping you see yourself through a new lens of love and sacredness. Her thoughtful, guided exercises are transformative and will gently reconnect you with the divine essence of who you are."

~Jenny Harkleroad, Founder of Balanced You

"You were never broken. You were always sacred." These words from Tiffany Cano's book have always inspired me.

As a psychologist and someone who has done deep inner work, I found this book to be a transformative guide. Tiffany gently leads you through body shame, generational wounds, and self-criticism, helping you reconnect with your worth and your sacredness. Her voice is both wise and nurturing, offering not just insight, but true soul nourishment.

I've been mentored by Tiffany since 2016, and her influence has been life-changing—both personally and professionally. Her work has helped me become a more loving mother, a more grounded therapist, and a more empowered woman. Because of her, I've been able to support my clients with greater depth and authenticity.

This isn't just a book—it's a healing journey. If you're ready to stop shrinking and start shining, Sacred Body Sacred Soul will meet you with love, truth, and transformation."

With Unity, Love & Respect,

Dr.

Maribel Contreras, Psy.D, LMFT

CEO of LifeForce Recovery Inc

If you or someone you love is a frontline hero in need of therapy or support, contact Life Force Recovery, Inc. — restoring strength and rebuilding lives at LifeForcerecovery@gmail.com or 213-322-6192

Part I: Reclaiming Your Body

1: Welcome Home to Yourself

2: Your Worth is Not Your Appearance

3: Beyond the Thin Ideal

4: Trusting Your Own Voice

5. Shifting from Punishment to Nourishment

6. Evolving Through Acceptance

Chapter 1: Welcome Home to Yourself — An Invitation into Sacred Body, Sacred Soul

There's a tender moment that happens in almost every healing circle I lead.

It's not the first tear, or the first story shared. It's the moment when someone exhales—the deep kind of exhale you didn't realize you were holding—and you can feel them softening into the safety of the space.

A subtle but powerful shift: from guarding to opening. From protecting to receiving.

From surviving ... to belonging.

That moment is what I want for you as you enter the pages of this book.

This isn't just a collection of words. *Sacred Body, Sacred Soul* is a sacred container—a healing field woven between you, me, and the Divine—to help you remember:

You are not broken.
You are not too far gone.
You are not alone.

> ## You are a Soul...
>
> **who came here in a body to experience love, belonging, radiance & truth.**

And even if you've been hurt …
Even if you've been carrying shame …
Even if you've forgotten how to feel safe in your own skin …
You can come home to yourself again.

Why This Journey Matters

I know firsthand how courageous it is to step onto the path of healing. It asks you to touch places you might have buried long ago. It invites you to meet not just the light, but the grief, the anger, the tenderness, the parts that once learned to survive by hiding.

That's why I want to name this before we begin:

Healing isn't always neat.

It can stir discomfort. Old memories. New emotions.

And it's okay.

Discomfort is not a sign that you're doing it wrong.

Discomfort is evidence that something sacred inside you is waking up.

This book is an invitation to walk through that discomfort with compassion, wisdom, and gentleness.

You will not be asked to rush, bypass, or fix yourself.

You will be invited to *befriend* yourself more deeply than ever before.

Every chapter was written with care to guide you through the layers of shame, fear, mistrust, and pain that sometimes live in the body, and to offer you tools, reflections, and practices that help you restore the truth that:

You were never meant to carry shame throughout your body.

Your body is sacred.

And your soul has always been holy.

A Little About Me

You might be wondering, Who is walking with me through this journey?

My name is Tiffany Cano, and for as long as I can remember, I have felt a calling to help people heal—body, mind, and soul.

I began my journey as a healer when I was just a child, offering comfort and energy healing long before I had formal words for it. Since then, I've dedicated 30 years to studying and practicing dozens of healing modalities, including neuroscience, trauma work, energy clearing, intuitive development, and subconscious reprogramming.

I've worked with thousands of empaths, intuitives, healers, and survivors from around the world, helping them see and heal the blind spots that were blocking their freedom, self-love, and ability to receive.

In my private sessions, group programs, and retreats, my greatest joy has been helping people feel safe enough to finally come home to themselves.

I am also in a series of upcoming *Transformation Movie Documentaries* to uplift and empower you. Be sure to catch them on major streaming platforms:

Pillars of Power: Discovering the Hidden Secrets Behind Achieving Greatness (Releasing Fall 2025)

Frequency of Miracles: Discover the Universes Secret to Success (Releasing Fall 2025)

Rise of the Lioness: The Power of Feminine Leadership (Releasing 2026)

Because true healing isn't about erasing your past. It's about *reclaiming* the parts of you that were never broken to begin with. That's the journey we're about to take together.

Setting the Sacred Space

Before you move forward, I want you to feel the safety of this container.

You are free to move at your own pace.

There is no "behind" here. No race to finish.

There is only presence. Only kindness.

You are allowed to:

- Take breaks when needed.
- Skip chapters and return later.
- Pause to breathe, cry, dance, laugh, journal, or pray.
- Allow yourself to let go and empty all that no longer serves.
- Come as you are.

If, at any point, a memory, emotion, or resistance arises, pause and tend to yourself.

Place a hand over your heart, breathe, and remind yourself:

> *"I am safe now. I have a choice now. I am not alone."*

You may wish to light *a **candle*** before reading.

Play soft music. Wrap yourself in a blanket.

Write down your reflections. This book is designed with space for you to pour your thoughts, beliefs, and feelings. Or, if you prefer, please choose a journal that you love.

Create a sacred atmosphere that reminds your body: *This is a safe place to feel.*

What You'll Experience Here

Each chapter will walk you through a subconscious block that may be living quietly in your body or psyche, shaping how you feel about yourself without you even realizing it.

We will explore:

- The hidden roots of body shame
- Healing internalized blame and guilt
- Restoring trust between you and your body
- Reclaiming sensuality and safe visibility
- Releasing inherited patterns of fear and unworthiness
- And so much more

Every chapter includes:

- **A heart-centered client story** (fictional-based on a composite of stories, subconscious thoughts, and energies of people who have struggled with similar subconscious blocks)
- **A healing affirmation** to anchor a new belief
- **Embodiment and energy practices** to reconnect to yourself

- **Reflection journal prompts** to deepen your self-awareness

You will not only read—you will *experience*.
You will not only think—you will *feel*.
You will not only remember—you will *reclaim*.
This is not just information—it is *transformation*.

To help you track your level of transformation, I invite you to take a self-assessment now and then after you have finished the book.

You Deserve to Feel Safe in Your Own Skin

You were never meant to:

- Apologize for your existence
- Shrink to make others comfortable
- Hide your beauty, your joy, your radiance
- Be punished for your softness
- Doubt your body's wisdom

You were meant to:

- Take up *space*
- Feel at *home* in your skin
- Move with *freedom* and *grace*

Sacred Body, Sacred Soul

Self-Reflection Scale

Please Rate Yourself (1–10 scale)

.... I feel safe and at home in my body.

.... I treat myself with compassion and kindness.

.... I feel comfortable being seen and taking up space.

.... I trust my body's wisdom and signals.

.... I feel worthy of love regardless of how I look.

.... I have healthy boundaries with others and myself.

.... I feel connected to my sacred feminine/masculine essence.

.... I honor my emotions without judgment.

.... I feel confident in my sensuality or softness.

.... I believe I am already whole.

- Express your *sensuality* without fear

- *Trust* yourself deeply and unshakably
- Remember that you are the *Soul,* having a human experience.

This isn't self-help.

This is soul-retrieval.

This is body reverence.

This is coming home.

Color In
Your
Current
Level
of
Satisfaction

Love Life

Sleep

Energy

Family

Health

Social

Work

Happiness

Play

Spiritual

1 = low
10 = high

Sacred Reading Agreement

I honor my own pace.

I am allowed to move slowly, linger, and return as often as needed.

I create a safe space for my emotions.
All feelings are welcome here—grief, joy, anger, hope.
None are wrong. All are sacred.

I tend lovingly to my body and nervous system.
If overwhelm arises, I pause.
I choose compassion over force.

I celebrate my growth.
Every small shift, every breath of courage, is a victory.

I remember that healing is possible for me.
I am not too broken.
I am not too late.
I am worthy of wholeness.

I am sacred.
I am sovereign.
I am home.

And so it is.

_____   _____
Your Name   Date

A Personal Invitation from My Heart to Yours

If you take nothing else away from this book, let it be this:

You are not too broken to heal.

You are not too far behind to reclaim yourself.

You are not too much, and you have never been not enough.

Your healing is not a fantasy.

It is your birthright.

It is already happening inside you, even now.

Let each chapter be a hand extended toward you.

Let each practice be a thread stitching your soul back into your body.

Let each affirmation be a prayer reminding you: *You were made sacred.*

Thank you, God, for facilitating healing on all levels. May negative, old energies, traumas, and beliefs that no longer serve be cleared and emptied out. Lord, also help to cultivate strong, healthy boundaries, bravery, and a sacred, safe, energetic container to be with any thoughts and emotions that come up.

Highly Perceptive People Academy

And if, along the way, you need deeper support, know that you don't have to walk alone.

My healing work continues beyond these pages.

Whether through 1:1 sessions, online programs, healing retreats, or our global Highly Perceptive People Academy community, you are welcome.

https://HighlyPerceptivePeopleAcademy.com

Want even more support, free gifts while you read this book? Pick up your bonus gifts to accompany you on your healing journey at

Sacred Body, Sacred Soul Bonus Gifts

www.SacredBodySacredSoul.com.

You are worthy of deep, embodied healing.

And I am honored to hold space for you.

I Am Here, With You ...

So take a breath with me now.

Feel your feet on the ground.

Feel the slow rise and fall of your chest.

Feel the beating of your beautiful, resilient heart.

You are here.

You are safe.

You are sacred.

And this journey—*your journey*—is just beginning.

Welcome home to your Sacred Body, Sacred Soul.

 *A Blessing*

May each page you turn be a hand reaching out to you.

May each breath you take be a bridge back home to your body.

May each moment of tenderness remind you:

You are healing.

You are radiant.

You are already whole.

With Love,

Tiffany

A companion on your sacred journey

Chapter 2: Reclaiming Worth Beyond Appearance

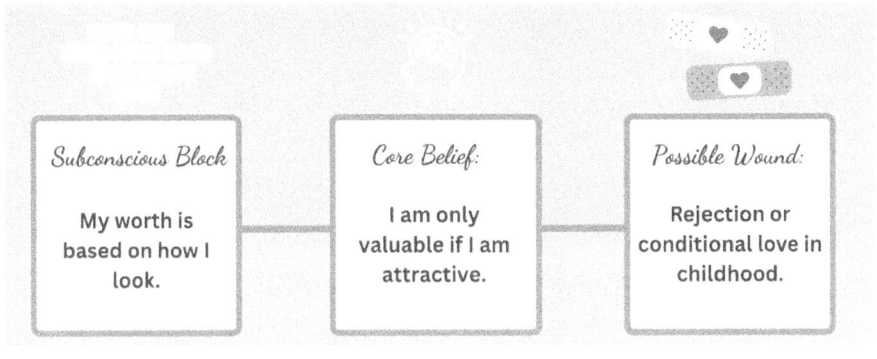

Subconscious Block	Core Belief:	Possible Wound:
My worth is based on how I look.	I am only valuable if I am attractive.	Rejection or conditional love in childhood.

When Karissa came into my workshop, she was radiant, but she couldn't see it.

On the outside, she appeared confident, successful, and composed. But in our first session, her truth came pouring out. "I feel like I'm constantly performing," she admitted. "I dress up, wear makeup, keep everything together… and yet, I still feel unworthy. Like I have to earn approval every single day." Her voice cracked as she continued, "If I'm not beautiful, I'm invisible."

That's the moment her eyes welled with tears, and I knew we had touched the root.

This belief—*that our worth is tied to how we look*—is one of the deepest and most painful illusions I see in the empathic women I work with. It's rarely spoken aloud, but it's there... whispering in the background of our thoughts. Shaping how we show up. Driving how we care for—or punish—our bodies. And creating an exhausting cycle of never feeling "enough."

Where the Wound Begins

Karissa grew up in a family where appearance was emphasized. Her mother, though well-meaning, often praised her only when she was "put together." Compliments came with conditions: "You look so pretty in that dress," or "You've lost weight—you look amazing!" The silence that followed when she didn't meet those standards spoke volumes.

In childhood, we learn to associate love with what gets attention. For Karissa, love and attention were linked to being attractive. If she looked good, she felt noticed and safe. If not, she felt invisible, disconnected, or even rejected.

This wound took root early, and it shaped how she related to herself for years. Her body became something to fix, manage, or use to gain approval. And any change—aging, weight fluctuations, breakouts, exhaustion—felt like a threat to her value.

This isn't unique to Karissa. It's a reflection of what so many empathic, intuitive, heart-centered people internalize in a world that values performance over presence and packaging over essence.

How It Shows Up

This subconscious belief might show up as:

- Feeling confident *only* when you're "put together"
- Avoiding mirrors or obsessively checking them
- Constant comparison with others
- Feeling like your value decreases if your body changes
- Seeking validation from social media likes or partner compliments
- A harsh inner critic that calls you lazy, messy, or not enough when you rest or show up "as you are"

One client said, "Even on my most peaceful days, I feel guilty if I don't look 'presentable.' Like I'm not allowed to just *be.*"

Can you relate?

The Shift Begins with Awareness

When we bring this belief to light, we can begin to unhook from it.

I asked Karissa one powerful question:

> *"Who would you be if you didn't have to prove your worth through how you look?"*

She was quiet for a moment. Then she said, "Free. I'd feel free."

That was the opening we needed. From there, we worked with somatic healing to release shame stored in her body. We explored inner child memories where she first learned this belief. We rewrote those stories and reconnected her to her soul's truth—that she was inherently worthy.

Over time, she began to *feel* different in her body. She started dressing for joy instead of approval. She moved her body in ways that felt nourishing, not punishing. And slowly, she began to look in the mirror and see herself with compassion instead of criticism.

She later shared:

> *"I looked at myself in the mirror today and didn't pick myself apart. I actually smiled. I'm beginning to see the light in me again. Thank you for helping me find my way home."*

Let's Begin That Journey Together

You don't have to wait until your body changes to love yourself.

You don't need to fix anything to feel worthy of rest, of love, of peace, of presence.

You are allowed to show up as you are—messy, radiant, soft, evolving.

Your worth is your birthright.

Healing Affirmation

Affirmation

**I am worthy and lovable exactly as I am.
My value is beyond my appearance.**

Say this aloud now. Whisper it into your heart. Breathe it in as truth.

Let it feel uncomfortable, if it needs to. That's okay. Truth sometimes stirs what's been asleep.

Healing Practice: Mirror Connection Ritual

Do this for the next 3 days:

1. Stand in front of a mirror, and look into your own eyes.
2. Place a hand on your heart or cheek.
3. Say aloud:

   "I see you. I love you. You are enough."

Notice what emotions come up. You don't need to judge them—just observe. This practice re-patterns the way you relate to your reflection. It creates a new, loving bond between you and your body.

Optional: Write a love letter to the version of you who always thought she had to earn love through beauty. Let her know she's safe now.

⊚ *Embodied Exercise: Worthiness Breathwork (5 min)*

1. Inhale deeply through the nose for 4 counts.
2. Hold for 4 counts.
3. Exhale slowly through the mouth for 6 counts.
   As you breathe, repeat:

   *Inhale: "I receive my **worth**."*
   Exhale: "I release the need to prove."

Let your body soften into the truth of who you already are.

📓 *Journal Reflections*

Take your time with going within to reflect and answer these questions:

In what ways have I measured my worth by appearance?

_____

_____

_____

_____

_____

Where did I first learn that looking good = being good or lovable?

_____

_____

_____

_____

What would shift if I believed I was inherently worthy, without conditions?

_____

_____

_____

_____

What do I admire in others that has *nothing* to do with how they look? Can I offer that same lens to myself?

_____

_____

_____

_____

_____

 *Gentle Reminder*

As a healer, I've witnessed hundreds of women unlearn the lie that their beauty defines their worth. And I want to remind you:

Your body is not a project to be perfected.

You are not more lovable when you weigh less, or wear more makeup, or post the perfect selfie.

You are lovable now. Exactly as you are.

Let this chapter be your turning point—not to become someone else, but to come home to *you.*

You are already enough.

You always were.

Chapter 3: You are Lovable as You Are

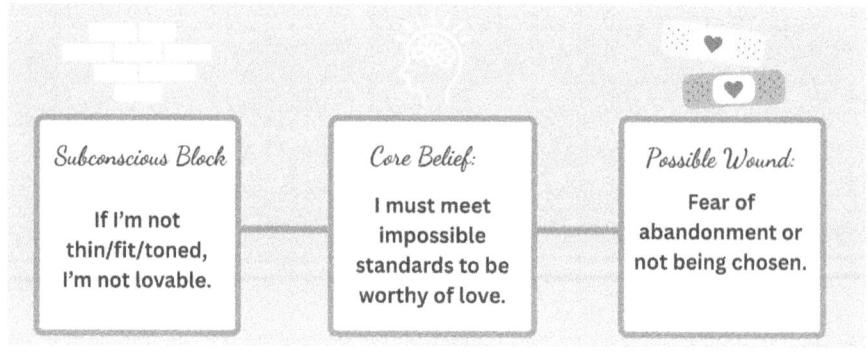

Subconscious Block	Core Belief:	Possible Wound:
If I'm not thin/fit/toned, I'm not lovable.	I must meet impossible standards to be worthy of love.	Fear of abandonment or not being chosen.

When Jamie first reached out to me, she was in tears.

Not because of a specific number on the scale or a single moment of judgment, but because she was *tired*. Tired of performing, tired of trying to "fix" her body, tired of believing that love lived on the other side of perfection.

"If I could just lose another ten pounds," she whispered, "maybe I'd finally feel like enough."

This belief—that love must be earned through effort and aesthetics—is one of the most deeply ingrained myths we carry, especially as empaths. So many of us grew up equating love with performance. With thinness. With attractiveness. With being "easy to love."

Jamie's story echoed that pattern. Her father, though present, was emotionally reserved. She remembered gaining a little weight around age 11 and how the teasing started. "You're getting pudgy," he'd say, only half-joking. "Better be careful—boys don't like that."

It was subtle, but it stuck. That tiny seed of shame grew alongside her.

Later, in high school, her first boyfriend used affection like currency. "You looked better before," he'd comment when she gained a few pounds. "You should wear tighter clothes—you're sexy when you try."

And so Jamie tried.

She became the girl who knew how to look "put together."

The girl who could control her hunger and push through workouts even when exhausted.

The girl who smiled wide but never truly felt seen.

Underneath it all, she was just a young woman who wanted to feel loved for her *soul*, not her shape.

The Cost of Conditional Love

In our early sessions, Jamie and I gently explored where this belief began—not just in memory, but in her *body*. Shame has a way of living in our cells. It tightens the belly, hunches the shoulders, constricts the breath. And, over time, it disconnects us from the very body we're trying to change.

When I asked Jamie to place her hands on her abdomen and speak kindly to it, she froze.

"It feels … wrong," she said. "Like it doesn't deserve kindness yet."

That's the wound.

That place where love has been postponed—until we shrink, until we tone, until we're "better."

But here's the truth I offered Jamie, and the one I offer you now:

   You do not need to shrink to be worthy of love.

   You do not need to earn softness, touch, or tenderness.

   You are already enough, right here, in the body you have today.

The Turning Point

As we continued working together, Jamie began reconnecting with her younger self—the girl who first started dieting at age 12, the one who stopped dancing because she felt too big, the one who longed for someone to say, "You are beautiful, no matter what."

We practiced inner child healing. I guided her through visualizations where she could hold that version of herself, speak affirming words, and offer the love she never received.

Slowly, the hard edges around her body began to soften.

One day, she went to the beach with her children. And for the first time in decades, she wore a bathing suit without covering up.

> *"I laughed," she told me later. "I played with my kids. I didn't once think about sucking in my stomach. I felt free."*

That, to me, is the real success story—not a body transformation, but a *belief* transformation. The kind that changes how you live, love, and breathe inside your own skin.

Why This Belief is So Common

We live in a society that commodifies women's bodies. Where "thin = desirable = lovable" is silently preached through advertisements, movie scripts, and even the words of those we love.

For sensitive souls, this gets internalized quickly. We're intuitive, attuned, and often overly responsible for the emotions of others. So we learn to adapt, shapeshift, and conform—to be the version of ourselves we think will be accepted.

But that performance is never sustainable. And eventually, our spirit calls us home.

💜 Healing Affirmation

Affirmation

Love flows to me because of who I Am, the Soul.

✦ Healing Practice: Inner Child Mirror Ritual

You'll need a mirror, a quiet space, and a photo of your younger self if possible.

1. Stand in front of the mirror. Gently hold your photo or imagine yourself at a young, tender age.
2. Place a hand on your heart. Take a few slow, deep breaths. Allow your heart chakra to open up, as you smile at your heart.
3. Look into your own eyes and say:
4. "You never had to earn love.
5. You are **worthy**, exactly as you are.
6. I will not abandon you again."

Let your words be a balm. If tears come, let them. They are holy and healing.

Repeat this ritual daily for three days. Watch what shifts.

◎ *Embodiment Practice: Nourishing Movement Check-In*

Instead of asking "How can I burn calories today?" ask:

"How would my body love to be moved today?"

Then listen. Maybe it's a walk in nature. Maybe it's dancing barefoot in your living room. Maybe it's rest.

Let joy, not judgment, be the guide.

Journal Reflections

What beliefs have I *inherited* about thinness and love?

_____

_____

_____

_____

_____

When did I first feel that my body was a "problem" to solve?

_____

_____

_____

_____

_____

Who benefits when I believe I must earn love through perfection?

_____

_____

_____

_____

_____

What would change if I believed that love already lives inside me?

_____

_____

_____

_____

_____

A Note From My Heart to Yours

As a healer for empaths, intuitives, and soul-led women, I have held space for many tender hearts like yours—people who have spent years waiting for permission to feel lovable.

Let me offer it to you now.

💜 You have *always* been lovable.

💜 You don't need to be a smaller size to deserve bigger love.

💜 You don't have to fix yourself to be worthy of being seen, adored, or held.

Your softness is sacred. Your curves, your edges, your breath—they're all expressions of life through you.

You are not here to be a mannequin of perfection.

You are here to be a living, breathing, feeling *miracle*.

Let this be the chapter where you stop waiting to be worthy.

You are lovable.

Now. Always. Still.

Chapter 4: Trusting Your Own Voice

Subconscious Block	Core Belief:	Possible Wound:
Other people's opinions about my body are more important than my own.	My *Safety* comes from external approval.	Lack of validation or support for authentic expression.

When Leila first joined my group program, she said something that stayed with me:

> "I don't think I've ever trusted myself enough to know how I really feel about my body. I just go with what everyone else says. It's safer that way."

She had been praised her entire life for being agreeable—polite, polished, and pleasant. But under the surface, she was disconnected from her truth.

She didn't know what she liked to wear, what movement felt good in her body, or how she really wanted to express herself. She was constantly filtering her body image through the eyes of others—her mother, her friends, romantic partners, even strangers on the internet.

When we started working together, it became clear that Leila had learned to abandon her inner voice in exchange for approval. And like many empaths, she had done this for years without realizing it.

She told me, "I don't know where I end and others begin."

The Empath's Dilemma

If you're an empath, or highly sensitive person, you may have learned to navigate the world by being highly attuned to others' emotions and expectations. You might pick up on someone's disapproval, even if it's subtle or unspoken.

Over time, this can create a subconscious strategy: "If I please others, I'll stay safe. If I trust myself, I might be rejected."

This pattern often starts early. For Leila, it began at age nine. She overheard her mom talking to an aunt about her "chubby stage." It wasn't meant to be cruel, but it stung. That was the day she stopped dancing freely in the living room. The day she started scanning others' faces to see how she should feel about her body.

The Cost of Silencing Your Voice

In adulthood, Leila became the "yes girl." The one who wore what her boyfriend liked. The one who posed the right way in photos. The one who constantly changed her eating habits depending on who she was around.

But it wasn't sustainable. The disconnection created chronic anxiety, especially around food, clothes, intimacy, and being seen.

"I feel like I've never fully shown up as me," she confessed. "Because I don't trust that I'll be accepted."

And that's the heart of it: When we silence our own voice long enough, we forget we even *have* one.

Rebuilding Self-Trust

In our sessions, I gently guided Leila back to herself.

We started small. Each morning, she placed a hand on her heart and asked, "What do *I* need today?" Then she wrote the answer in a journal, even if it felt silly or simple.

She started experimenting with choosing outfits based on how they *felt* on her skin, not how they looked to others.

She stopped asking her partner, "Does this look okay?" and started asking herself, "Do *I* feel good in this?"

These subtle shifts built trust between her and her body. Day by day, she began reclaiming her voice.

And then, during one of our final sessions, she beamed and said:

> "I chose an outfit that felt like me and wore it with confidence. For the first time in years, I didn't shrink to fit someone else's preference. I **expanded**."

That's what this healing is about. Not just learning to love your body, but learning to *trust* your inner guidance and reclaim your power.

 Healing Affirmation

> *Affirmation*
>
> **My Voice Matters.**
> **I trust my inner voice more than the opinions of others.**

Say this aloud. Let the words settle into your chest, your belly, your bones.

If your inner child has been waiting a lifetime to hear this ... let her know you're listening now.

Healing Practice: The Mirror Voice Ritual

1. Stand in front of a mirror and look into your eyes—not to fix or evaluate, but to connect.
2. Place your hands on your heart or your womb.
3. Say slowly:

4. "I see you. I hear you. *Your voice matters.* Your truth is enough."
5. Pause. If tears come, let them. They are sacred and a great release.

Repeat this ritual once a day for three days. Observe how your energy shifts as your body begins to feel heard.

◎ *Energetic Alignment Practice: The "Me First" Check-In*

When you feel unsure or tempted to seek outside approval, try this:

- Pause.
- Close your eyes.
- Ask inwardly: "What feels right *for me*?"
- Breathe deeply. Let the answer rise from your body, not your mind.

This is how you build embodied trust—one choice, one breath, one truth at a time.

📓 Journal Reflections

Whose opinions about my body have I internalized over the years?

_____

_____

_____

_____

_____

What parts of myself have I silenced to fit in, stay safe, or be accepted?

_____

_____

_____

_____

_____

What does my intuition say when I stop trying to please everyone else?

_____

_____

_____

_____

_____

What would it look like to reclaim my preferences, my style, my way of being?

_____

_____

_____

_____

_____

A Love Note to the Empath Who Forgot Herself

My dear one, if you've spent a lifetime filtering your body image through the gaze of others, I want to say this gently and clearly:

- You are allowed to trust yourself.

- You are allowed to define your own beauty.

- You are allowed to speak your truth, even if it's different, messy, or still unfolding.

Your voice is not a threat. It's a gift.

And when you learn to trust it, you become the author of your own story, not the echo of someone else's.

This is the beginning of your sovereignty. Let it be the chapter where you stop performing and start embodying who you truly are.

You don't need to be perfect to be powerful.

You just need to be you.

Chapter 5: Releasing the Need to Punish Your Body

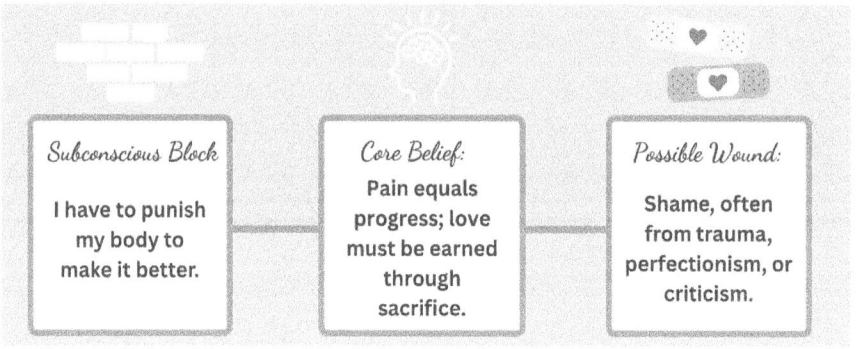

Subconscious Block	Core Belief:	Possible Wound:
I have to punish my body to make it better.	Pain equals progress; love must be earned through sacrifice.	Shame, often from trauma, perfectionism, or criticism.

When I met Brielle, she carried herself like a warrior. She was disciplined, efficient, and always striving toward the next level of achievement. On the outside, she appeared powerful, but on the inside, she was exhausted.

Her relationship with her body was built on control: counting calories, measuring macros, forcing workouts even when she was in pain. And yet, no matter how hard she tried, she never felt like she was enough.

"I feel like my body is always the enemy," she admitted one day. "I have to fight it. Control it. Push it. If I stop, everything will fall apart."

That belief—that the only way to feel proud is to suffer—was deeply rooted in her nervous system. And sadly, it's one I've seen in so many intuitive, empathic women who learned that love, success, and approval must be earned through self-sacrifice.

Where This Pattern Begins

For Brielle, it started in childhood. Her parents praised achievement, not presence. Her mother was constantly on diets. Her father admired discipline and toughness. Crying was a weakness. Rest was laziness. The body was something to manage—never something to trust.

By the time Brielle reached adulthood, she had internalized a clear message: *If I'm not working hard, especially at fixing my body, I'm failing.*

She lived in a cycle of overworking, overtraining, and perfectionism. Resting made her anxious. Eating intuitively felt dangerous. Pleasure was a luxury she didn't believe she deserved.

In one session, I asked, "What if you didn't have to suffer to be worthy?"

She paused, and then whispered, "That's a hard one. I'm not sure I know who I'd be without that struggle."

Why Empaths Learn to Punish Themselves

As empaths, many of us learned to take responsibility for the emotional energy around us. We became hyper-aware of how others felt, and somewhere along the way, we began to equate our ability to *carry* pain with being *good enough*.

For some, the body becomes the target of that pain. When we can't fix our circumstances or past, we try to fix our physical selves. When we feel powerless, we try to control our bodies. And when we're carrying unprocessed shame, we often turn that shame inward—punishing ourselves through neglect, restriction, overexertion, or self-criticism.

Brielle didn't hate her body; she hated the feeling of not being enough. Her body just became the battleground for that belief.

Shifting from Punishment to Partnership

The breakthrough came when I asked Brielle to consider a new possibility: *What if your body is your ally, not your enemy?*

We began the process of reconnecting her with her body—not as a machine to control, but as a sacred partner to nourish. We practiced somatic listening: placing a hand on her belly, asking what her body needed, and actually waiting for an answer.

At first, it felt awkward. "I don't hear anything," she said.

But a few sessions later, she said something different.

> "I asked my body what she needed, and I actually felt it. She wanted to rest. Not more reps. Not more restrictions. Just … rest."

That moment changed everything. It was the first time she chose love over punishment.

A New Way to Measure Progress

Progress isn't always visible on the surface. Sometimes, it looks like softening your inner voice. Sometimes, it's in the moment you skip the workout and take a bath without guilt. Sometimes, it's when you choose the meal that satisfies you, not the one that punishes you.

Brielle's story evolved beautifully.

A few months after our work began, she shared:

> "I still like goals. I still enjoy moving my body. But now, I check in before I act. I ask, 'Is this love or punishment?' I no longer punish my body into progress. I partner with my body temple."

That is sacred growth.

 Healing Affirmation

Affirmation

I nourish and move my body from a place of love.
I refrain from punishing myself.

Say it slowly. Let the energy of those words reach the parts of you that have been working too hard for too long. Let them remind you that you can rest now and still be worthy.

Healing Practice: Love or Punishment Body Check-In

Before any self-care activity (a workout, a food choice, a task), ask yourself:

- Am I doing this from *love* or punishment?
- Would I make the same choice if I already felt enough?

If it feels like punishment, pause. Breathe. Ask what your body actually needs in this moment.

You'll be amazed at how different self-care feels when it comes from love.

ⓢ *Somatic Exercise: The Body Blessing*

1. Find a quiet space. Light a candle or create a peaceful atmosphere.

2. Starting from your feet, place your hands on different areas of your body and gently speak a blessing aloud:

   - "I offer love to my feet. Thank you for grounding me."

   - "I offer love to my thighs. Thank you for carrying me forward."

   - "I offer love to my belly. Thank you for holding my life force."

   - Continue all the way up to the top of your head.

Don't rush. Let this become a ritual of reverence, not a task.

 *Journal Reflections*

What early experiences taught me that I had to work hard or suffer to be good enough?

_____

_____

_____

_____

_____

Where in my life am I still trying to earn love or worth through control?

_____

_____

_____

_____

_____

What would shift if I believed I was already enough, without doing, achieving, or pushing?

_____

_____

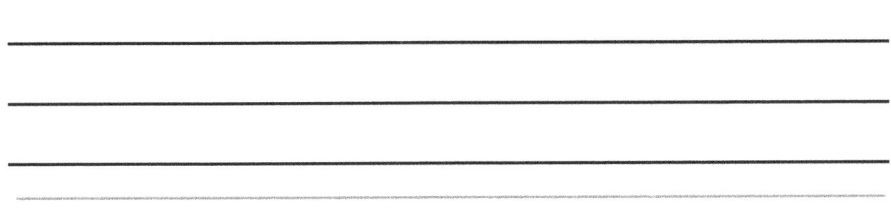

A Loving Reminder for the Overachiever

To the one who's always pushing … always striving … always hustling for her worth …

You don't need to prove your value by punishing your body.

Your softness is not weakness.

Your rest is not laziness.

And your body is not broken.

She is sacred. She is wise. She is waiting to be loved—not just when she reaches a goal, but now. Today. Exactly as she is.

This chapter is your permission slip to shift from control to compassion. From performance to presence. From punishment … to partnership.

You are allowed to be gentle with yourself.

You are allowed to rest.

You are allowed to heal.

Chapter 6: Evolving Through Self-Acceptance

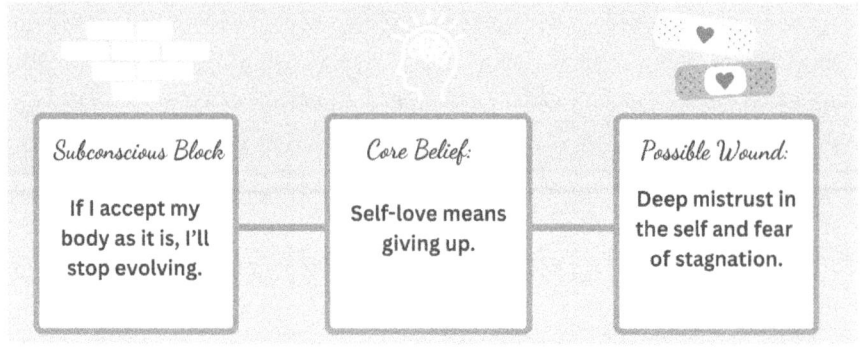

Subconscious Block	Core Belief:	Possible Wound:
If I accept my body as it is, I'll stop evolving.	Self-love means giving up.	Deep mistrust in the self and fear of stagnation.

"I'm afraid that if I stop pushing myself, I'll stop growing."

That was the first thing Tanya said to me in our private session.

She was sitting in front of me with impeccable posture, her planner open on the table, her jaw tight. Everything about her energy whispered, "I must hold it all together."

"I have to stay vigilant," she said. "I've worked so hard to change my body and improve myself. If I let up, I'll lose everything."

As she spoke, I felt the subtle tremble of fear beneath her control. This wasn't about laziness. It was about safety.

Tanya believed that self-acceptance meant complacency. That if she stopped striving, she would fall apart. She'd gained so much approval through being driven, self-critical, and disciplined. But it came at a cost. She was exhausted. Disconnected. And deep down, she was terrified that she was only lovable if she was evolving.

The Myth of Self-Acceptance as Surrender

This belief—that accepting ourselves means we'll stop growing—is one of the most stubborn and painful lies that perfectionism tells us.

Especially for empaths and intuitives who tend to carry early wounds of being "too much" or "not enough," the idea of resting in who we are can feel dangerous.

Tayna had been a high-achiever since childhood. Straight A's. Always composed. She internalized early that her value came from being the best version of herself—better than she was yesterday, never fully arriving.

Her parents praised her accomplishments but rarely celebrated her essence. Her body became a battleground of constant improvement: cleaner eating, harder workouts, more discipline.

In our sessions, we began peeling back the layers of this belief system with compassion. I asked her one day, "What do you think would happen if you loved your body just as she is?"

Tanya's eyes filled with tears.

"Honestly? I think I'd let myself go ... and no one would love me anymore."

There it was. The root wound: the fear that love is conditional and tied to constant bettering.

What Self-Acceptance Actually Is

Let's be clear: self-acceptance is not resignation.

It's not saying, "I guess this is all I'll ever be."

It's saying, "I choose to love and honor who I am in this moment ... even as I evolve."

True transformation isn't fueled by shame. It's fueled by safety. The more we accept and embrace ourselves as we are, the more space we create for authentic growth.

When Tanya finally allowed herself to sit in her softness—to rest, to be instead of do—she began healing from the inside out. Her nervous system calmed. Her choices became rooted in desire, not duty. Her relationship with her body shifted from battle to bond.

The Turning Point

One day, Tanya shared this story:

"I was getting dressed for an event and realized I usually choose clothes based on how flattering they are. But that day, I asked myself, 'What feels good on my body?'

I wore a dress I hadn't worn in years—not because it made me look smaller, but because it made me feel alive.

I didn't shrink. I didn't hide. I didn't apologize.

I accepted myself, and I felt radiant."

That's when I knew she was healing.

Because when self-acceptance takes root, evolution doesn't stop—it deepens.

💜 *Healing Affirmation*

Affirmation
Self-acceptance fuels my evolution.
Loving myself helps me grow.

Say this slowly. Let each word sink in. You are not falling behind by embracing who you are. You are coming home to the most powerful place of transformation.

✦ *Embodiment Practice: The Mirror of Enoughness*

This ritual gently reconditions the nervous system to feel safe in self-acceptance.

1. Stand in front of a mirror. Breathe slowly.

2. Look into your own eyes—not critically, but kindly.

3. Place your hands on your body—your heart, your belly, your arms. Any part of you that needs love.

4. Say aloud:

5. "In this moment, *I am enough.*

6. I do not need to change to be worthy of love.

7. I evolve from joy, and refrain from judgment."

Repeat this for 5 days. Journal anything that rises after each experience.

🌀 Somatic Exercise: Accept & Anchor Breathwork

This breathwork helps regulate your body's stress response around self-worth.

1. Inhale deeply for 4 counts, saying internally, "I *accept* myself."
2. Hold for 2 counts.
3. Exhale for 6 counts, saying, "I anchor in *love*."
4. Repeat for 5 cycles.

Do this daily, especially before making choices about your body, your work, or your appearance.

📓 Journal Reflections

What do I believe would happen if I truly accepted myself right now?

_____

_____

_____

_____

_____

Whose voice taught me that rest or softness = failure?

_____

_____

_____

_____

_____

How does striving keep me feeling safe?

_____

_____

_____

_____

_____

What part of me is ready to evolve from love, not lack?

_____

_____

_____

_____

_____

A Soft Reminder for the One Who's Been Working So Hard

Please let go of any thoughts that you need to fix yourself to be good enough.

You don't need to shrink, perfect, hustle, or prove.

You are allowed to stop running and start resting in the radiant truth of who you already are.

Evolution doesn't begin at the finish line. It begins the moment you say,

"I accept this version of me ... and she is already worthy of love."

Let this be your new rhythm: softening, not forcing. Listening, not striving.

Loving yourself into growth, not bullying yourself into submission.

You are already becoming.

And you are already enough.

Part II: Healing & Transmuting Internalized Shame

Chapter 7: From Problem to Partnership

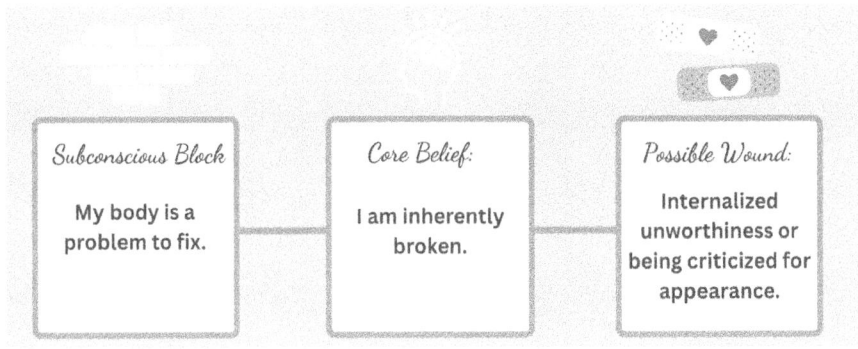

Subconscious Block	Core Belief:	Possible Wound:
My body is a problem to fix.	I am inherently broken.	Internalized unworthiness or being criticized for appearance.

When Rayna arrived at my workshop, she had a softness about her, but her energy was tightly guarded. She shared openly in our opening circle, though I could feel the ache behind her smile.

"I've spent my entire life trying to fix myself," she said. "Fix my weight. Fix my skin. Fix how I walk, how I talk, how I take up space. I've never once looked in the mirror and thought, 'You're okay just as you are.'"

Her voice cracked.

We all felt it.

Rayna was exhausted—not from life, but from the internal war she'd been waging against her own body for decades. She wasn't alone. I've met countless women in my healing spaces who believe their body is a problem, a puzzle, a project to manage. A burden to carry. Something that must be fixed before love, joy, or worth can be claimed.

The Moment It All Began

Rayna's earliest memory of body shame wasn't loud. It was subtle, like it often is for empaths.

She was eight years old, getting ready for a family photo. Her aunt commented on her dress, saying, "Maybe something more slimming would be better." It wasn't cruel, but it landed hard.

It taught her, in an instant, that her body was something to adjust, not celebrate.

From there, the messages multiplied. Weight-loss ads. Magazine covers. The ever-present comparison to thinner friends. Over time, she didn't just feel like her body was *different*—she believed her body was *wrong*.

This is how the "fixing" story begins. We learn to see our bodies through the lens of dissatisfaction. And slowly, that lens becomes the only one we trust.

The Hidden Pain of Being a "Project"

What Rayna expressed in that circle is something I've heard echoed by healers, mothers, CEOs, teachers, and teenagers alike:

> "I feel like I've been trying to fix my body for as long as I can remember."

It might show up like:

- Constantly researching diets, programs, or procedures
- Avoiding photos or hiding in oversized clothes
- Picking apart your body in the mirror before you've even taken a breath
- Feeling like your joy or confidence must be postponed until "after" the next change

When you believe your body is a problem, you stop seeing her as a living, sacred vessel, and instead treat her like a project to be micromanaged.

Shifting into Sacred Partnership

One of the first things I said to Rayna during our private session was this:

> "What if your body isn't a problem to solve … but a partner to support?"

She exhaled. Visibly.

The question bypassed her intellect and touched something ancient in her. Something that had been waiting—years, maybe lifetimes—to be loved.

That session, I guided her through a womb-healing meditation where she placed her hands on her belly and spoke to her body—not with demands, but with devotion.

> "I'm sorry I judged you. I'm sorry I ignored you.
>
> I'm willing to learn how to love you now."

It was tender. Tears streamed down her face. Her body, once seen as flawed, began to be felt as family.

Your Body is Not an Obstacle

Beloved, if you've carried the belief that your body is a mistake or a problem ... let me remind you:

- Your body is not in the way.
- Your body *is* the way.

Your body carries your spiritual essence and receives intuition. Your pleasure. Your power. Your stories. Your healing. Your beautiful body temple is not the thing to fix, so let this be the beginning of being present and available inside your body.

🩶 *Healing Affirmation*

> ### *Affirmation*
> **My body is sacred.**
> **I release the need to fix and choose to love.**

Say this with a hand on your heart and another on your belly.

Feel what shifts when you stop trying to correct and start offering compassion.

Healing Practice: The "Thank You" Ritual

When you begin seeing your body as a partner, gratitude becomes a healing tool.

Do this at the end of your day:

1. Sit or lie down comfortably. Take 3, slow, grounding breaths.
2. Out loud or silently, thank each part of your body:
   - *"Thank you,* feet, for carrying me."
   - *"Thank you,* thighs, for your strength."
   - *"Thank you,* belly, for holding life and emotion."
3. Keep going, even for 2-3 minutes.

4. End by whispering to yourself:

5. "You are not a problem. You are a blessing."

---

⑥ *Somatic Integration: "Softening the Critic"*

Next time you notice a harsh thought about your body, do this:

1. Pause and place a hand on the area you criticized.

2. Breathe into that space for a count of 4.

3. Say:

4. "I see you. I'm learning to love you."

5. "You don't have to change or be perfect to be worthy of my care."

Even if it feels fake at first, it's a seed. And seeds grow with gentleness.

📓 Journal Reflections

What moments from my past taught me that my body needed to be "fixed"?

_____

_____

_____

_____

_____

What have I postponed—joy, rest, confidence—until my body changed?

_____

_____

_____

_____

_____

What would it feel like to be in a relationship of *partnership* with my body?

_____

_____

_____

_____

_____

What qualities does my body hold that I am grateful for?

_____

_____

_____

_____

_____

_____

A Sacred Reframe for the Tender Parts of You

To the part of you that feels unworthy, unwanted, unseen …

To the part of you that has tried to fix, shrink, hide, and perfect …

Let this be the chapter where you stop seeing your body as a project and start treating her like a temple.

You don't need to *earn* the right to love your body. You just need to begin the conversation.

Even if it's clumsy. Even if it's unfamiliar. Even if your body isn't used to being spoken to with kindness.

This is a homecoming.

From fixing to *partnership*.

From control to *connection*.

From shame ... to *sacredness*.

You are not broken, love.

You are beautiful.

Let your healing begin from that truth.

Chapter 8: Embracing Joy Now

Subconscious Block	*Core Belief:*	*Possible Wound:*
I'll only be happy when I reach a certain weight or size.	Joy must be postponed until I'm "perfect."	Conditional self-acceptance and deferred self-love.

When my client Noelle came to me, she was deeply spiritual, emotionally aware, and so kind to everyone … except for herself.

"I just want to feel confident," she said during our intake session. "But every time I start to feel good, I remember I'm not where I want to be yet. I tell myself, 'You can feel proud when you lose weight.' Until then, it's like I don't have permission to be happy."

She wasn't trying to be harsh—she honestly believed she had to "earn" her happiness.

And she's not alone.

This subconscious block—the belief that joy, love, confidence, and even self-expression must wait until we "fix" ourselves—is heartbreakingly common. Especially among empaths and intuitives who've learned to tie their worth to other people's expectations or societal ideals of beauty.

The Illusion of the "After" Life

Noelle kept chasing an imagined version of herself:

- The version that finally lost the weight
- The version who didn't have cellulite
- The version who felt "put together" all the time

She believed that once she arrived at that version of herself, *then* she could go on dates, wear that dress, take the trip, or feel sexy in her own skin.

It's a belief I call "The After Illusion."

It says, *"Once I get there, then I'll be enough. Then I'll deserve to enjoy my life."*

But here's the quiet heartbreak: Many people never get "there," and even if they do, they still don't feel free. Because the belief that they must earn happiness was never healed.

Where This Block Begins

For Noelle, it started when she was twelve. She got a new outfit she adored, but when she showed it to her mother, the response was, "You'll look even better in that once you slim down."

One sentence. One moment. A seed planted.

From then on, Noelle linked celebration with condition. Joy had to be justified. She internalized the idea that it wasn't safe to feel proud until she was smaller, prettier, more disciplined.

So, even as an adult, she postponed pleasure. She wouldn't buy clothes she loved, or enjoy photos of herself, or dance in public ... not until she "deserved it."

But what she didn't realize was this: *postponed joy becomes grief.*

Reclaiming Joy in the Present Moment

I asked Noelle a question I often ask my clients:

"What would it feel like to stop waiting?"

Her eyes filled with tears.

"Honestly ... I wouldn't know how to be with myself.
I've been waiting my whole life."

That's when we began her return to joy—not later, not someday, but *now*.

Together, we practiced what I call *micro-moments of celebration*—learning to welcome joy in small, daily ways. Not because she reached a goal, but because she was *already worthy*.

We began with things like:

- Wearing a dress she loved, even if she didn't feel "ready"
- Taking selfies that captured joy, not perfection
- Saying yes to experiences that her "after" self would have enjoyed

And slowly, she began to feel alive again.

The Breakthrough

One day, Noelle messaged me a photo. She was at the beach, wind in her hair, wearing a bright coral swimsuit.

She wrote:

> "I almost didn't go. I didn't feel 'ready.' But I kept hearing your voice: *You don't have to wait to feel beautiful.*
> I went. I played in the waves. I laughed so hard I cried. And for the first time in years … I felt free."

That's what reclaiming joy looks like. It's not about abandoning growth—it's about honoring the *truth* that your joy doesn't have to wait for perfection.

💜 Healing Affirmation

Affirmation
Joy is available to me now.
I choose to feel good in my body today.

Say this now, aloud or silently. Say it to your reflection. Say it to your inner child. Say it until your nervous system begins to believe that celebration is safe.

✦ Healing Practice: The Joy Reclamation List

1. Grab your journal and create two columns.
    - Column A: "Things I've Been Waiting to Do"
    - Column B: "How I Can Begin Today"
2. Under Column A, write down the things you've put off until you lose weight, reach a goal, or feel more confident.
3. Then, for each item, ask: *How can I say yes to this now, even in a small way?*

Examples:

Things I've Been Waiting to Do		*How I Can Begin Today*
Waiting to wear color		Buy or wear one colorful piece now
Waiting to go on a date		Plan a solo self-love date first
Waiting to dance		Dance in your kitchen tonight
Waiting to _____		Action: _____
Waiting to _____		Action: _____

4. Take one action from Column B this week. Celebrate it. No shrinking. No shame.

◉ *Embodiment Practice: Celebration Activation*

Music is a powerful portal to joy. Try this simple practice:

1. Choose a song that makes you feel radiant or alive.
2. Play it loud.
3. Let your body move. Not for performance—just for *pleasure*.
4. Smile at yourself in the mirror as you move.
5. Whisper or sing:
6. "I am allowed to enjoy this body. *I am allowed to feel joy.*"

Do this for five minutes a day for one week. Notice what shifts.

📓 Journal Reflections

What have I been waiting to do until I "feel ready"?

_____

_____

_____

_____

_____

Who taught me that joy must be earned through appearance or achievement?

_____

_____

_____

_____

_____

What would it feel like to experience joy now, as I am?

_____

_____

_____

_____

_____

What is one joyful thing I can say yes to today?

_____

_____

_____

_____

_____

A Message for the One Who's Been Waiting

You don't have to earn your joy.

You don't need to weigh less, wear more, or work harder to deserve the life you want.

Joy is not a reward—it's a right. And your body is not an obstacle to pleasure; it's the vessel for it.

You are allowed to be happy now.

To take the photo. Wear the outfit. Say yes to the adventure.

You don't have to apologize for your joy. And you don't have to wait.

Let this be the chapter where you stop deferring your dreams.

You are not a "before" version of yourself.

You are already someone worth celebrating.

Now is sacred.

Now is enough.

Now is yours.

Chapter 9: Trusting Cravings and Intuition

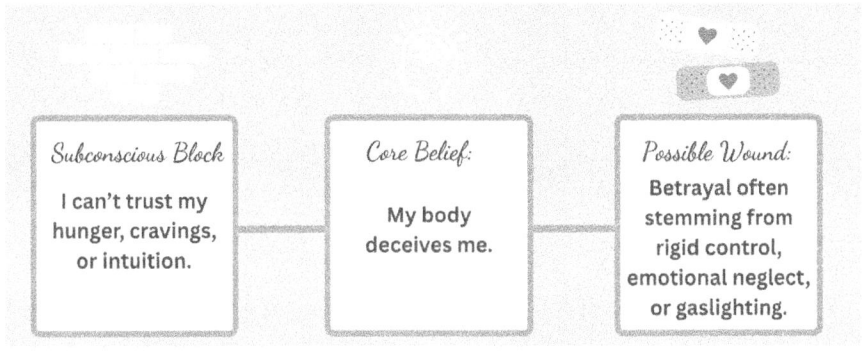

Subconscious Block	Core Belief:	Possible Wound:
I can't trust my hunger, cravings, or intuition.	My body deceives me.	Betrayal often stemming from rigid control, emotional neglect, or gaslighting.

Tara came into our work with a bright smile, but a tangled relationship with her body's desires.

She had spent most of her adult life believing her cravings were the enemy. "If I listen to my hunger," she said in our first session, "I'll spiral. I'll lose control. I'll never stop." She said it with such conviction that I could hear the years of internal war behind her words.

Tara wasn't just talking about food. She didn't trust her body's *hunger* for anything—rest, pleasure, even guidance. Cravings felt dangerous. Intuition felt unreliable. She'd learned to override her body's signals in the name of safety.

And yet, beneath all that control lived a soul craving one thing more than anything else: *permission to trust herself.*

Where This Disconnect Begins

Tara's story began when she was young. Her family praised self-control and discipline above all else. Emotions weren't talked about. Desires were seen as weaknesses. If she was hungry, she was told to wait. If she cried, she was told to stop. If she wanted something for herself, it was selfish.

Slowly, she internalized the belief that her body's signals couldn't be trusted.

By the time she was in college, she was excellent at ignoring herself—ignoring hunger cues, ignoring exhaustion, ignoring instincts that whispered *no* when people crossed her boundaries. She could quote every nutrition label but couldn't tell when she was full. She could power through a packed schedule but couldn't feel when her body was begging for rest.

She had disconnected so deeply from her body that even when it whispered in the language of fatigue, longing, or gut-feelings, she couldn't hear it.

The Empath's Betrayal Pattern

This block is especially common for empaths. As highly attuned beings, many of us were never taught how to interpret our own energetic signals. Instead, we learned to override them in favor of external guidance, spiritual logic, or survival programming.

You may relate if you've ever:

- Ignored hunger until it became unbearable
- Second-guessed your gut feelings in relationships
- Believed that cravings made you weak or broken
- Confused emotional hunger for physical needs
- Felt guilt for wanting food, pleasure, or time alone

When you've experienced trauma, neglect, or control, your body's voice can feel *untrustworthy.* And that's not your fault—it's a protective pattern.

But it *can* be healed.

Coming Back to the Body

With Tara, we began the gentle process of body re-attunement.

I invited her into small, sacred moments of listening. Before each meal, instead of asking, *"What's healthy?"* she asked, *"What do I really want?"* At first, it terrified her. "If I let myself eat what I want," she said, "I'll eat everything."

But here's what happened: when she gave herself permission, the chaos began to soften. The binge-urge dissolved. She found herself craving things she hadn't tasted in years—not out of rebellion, but reverence.

One evening, she sent me a voice message.

> "I made pasta. Real pasta. Not zucchini noodles. I ate slowly. I actually tasted it. And I stopped when I felt satisfied—not stuffed, just … whole. I didn't think I was capable of that."

That's what happens when we bring *presence* into our cravings. They become sacred invitations, not sources of shame.

Cravings as Divine Messengers

Here's what I teach my clients: *cravings are communication.*

- When you crave sugar, your body may be asking for *sweetness in your life.*
- When you crave rest, it might be because *your nervous system is overextended.*
- When your intuition says *no* and you ignore it, *the body responds with anxiety.*

Your body doesn't lie. It simply reflects the truth you've been taught to silence.

Healing begins by learning the language of your own being again.

 Healing Affirmation

Affirmation
I trust my body's wisdom.
My cravings and intuition are sacred messengers.

Say this with one hand on your womb and the other hand on your heart. Let the affirmation become a quiet song inside your cells.

Healing Practice: The Sacred Craving Pause

Next time you feel a craving—food, rest, movement, touch—pause before acting.

Ask yourself:

- "What am I really hungry for?"
- "What is this desire trying to show me?"
- "If I trusted my body, what would I do now?"

No judgment. Just curiosity. Let this be the beginning of listening again.

🌀 *Embodiment Practice: Intuition Reconnection Walk*

1. Take a short walk without your phone or distractions.
2. With each step, breathe deeply into your belly.
3. Ask yourself one question you've been struggling with.
4. Then … just walk. Don't analyze.
5. Let the rhythm of your body create space for answers to rise.

Trust that your body already knows. You're not looking for *logic*—you're listening for *alignment*.

 *Journal Reflections*

What messages did I receive growing up about hunger or desire?

_____

_____

_____

_____

_____

When have I ignored or overridden my body's wisdom?

_____

_____

_____

_____

What cravings keep showing up for me, and what might they be pointing to?

_____

_____

_____

_____

Where can I invite more trust into my relationship with my body and intuition?

_____

_____

_____

_____

_____

A Message for the One Learning to Listen Again

Beloved …

You are not broken. You are not weak. You are not out of control.

You are awakening.

What looks like craving is often just your body trying to get your attention.

What feels like chaos is usually unexpressed wisdom, finally asking to be heard.

You don't need to earn the right to trust yourself.

You *were born* with the ability to know what you need.

Let this be the chapter where you begin again—not with rules, but with reverence. Not with fear, but with faith in the temple of your own body.

She remembers.

And so will you.

Chapter 10: Honoring the Body's Journey

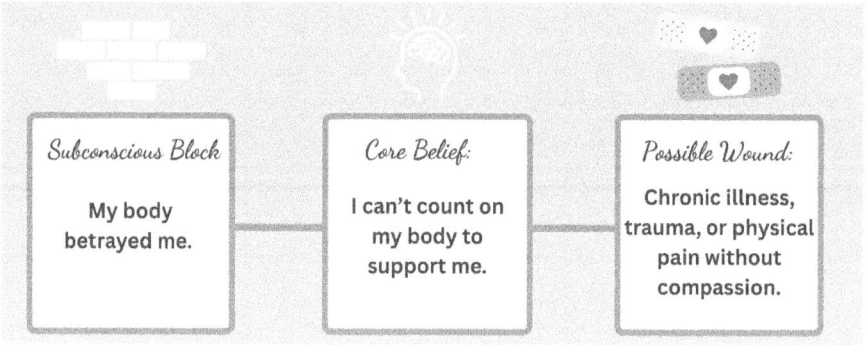

Subconscious Block	Core Belief:	Possible Wound:
My body betrayed me.	I can't count on my body to support me.	Chronic illness, trauma, or physical pain without compassion.

Lauren sat across from me on Zoom, her voice quiet, but her pain loud.

"I used to feel proud of my body," she said, "but after the miscarriage … everything changed. I felt like it failed me. Like it turned against me." Her hands trembled slightly as she spoke. "I haven't been able to trust it since. I don't even know if I want to."

This chapter is for every person who's felt abandoned by their body, whether through illness, injury, trauma, or an experience like Lauren's—something unexpected and heartbreaking that changed the way they viewed their physical self.

When what was once familiar becomes foreign. When the body becomes a source of grief, not grounding. When something goes "wrong" and the mind doesn't just question the body, it condemns it.

The Wound of Betrayal

Lauren's story isn't uncommon. I, too, have lost a baby and know the pain, confusion, betrayal and loss. And I've worked with many women whose relationships with their bodies changed not because of external appearance, but because of internal rupture.

Some shared about autoimmune conditions, others about hormonal imbalances, unexplained pain, or surgeries that altered their sense of identity. One client described her fibromyalgia diagnosis as "the day I lost faith in my body." Another, who survived sexual assault, said, "I blamed my body for not fighting back. For freezing."

This subconscious belief—*"My body betrayed me"*—is incredibly tender. And it deserves a kind of healing that goes beyond positive thinking. It requires restoration. Reunion. Rebuilding trust where it's been broken.

Reframing the Story

In Lauren's case, we worked together over a few months to gently separate the grief of her loss from the shame directed at her body. Through guided visualizations, energy work, and energy healing to release the miscarriage trauma, she began to open up to a new possibility:

What if the body didn't fail?

What if it responded the only way it knew how?

What if instead of being the villain of the story, the body was the one who needed holding?

This shift didn't come overnight. But it began with one core truth I offered her and now offer to you:

> *Your body didn't betray you. Your body is still trying to protect you.*

Even if your body shut down. Even if it got sick. Even if it couldn't do what you needed at the time. Your body responded from survival, not sabotage.

The Body Remembers, and So Can You

When trust is lost—especially in something as intimate as your own body—the healing process begins with remembering:

- That your body has carried every heartbreak *and kept going*.
- That your lungs *kept breathing* through anxiety.
- That your legs *still moved*, even when you felt paralyzed by fear.

- That your heartbeat *never abandoned* you, even when hope did.

The body isn't against you. It's just been carrying more than it was ever meant to carry alone.

What Lauren Learned to See Differently

Through our healing journey, Lauren began to speak *to* her body instead of *about* it. One exercise that opened her heart was writing a *forgiveness letter* to her womb. At first, it was full of anger. Blame. Hurt. But slowly, compassion found its way in.

Weeks later, she wrote:

> *"I thought you let me down. But now I see you held my grief. You held my hope. You never turned away from me. I turned away from you."*

It was the beginning of reconnection. Not just with her body but with herself.

 Healing Affirmation

Affirmation

I honor my body's journey.
We are healing together with compassion.

Repeat this as often as needed, especially when old stories try to rise again. Let it anchor you in the truth that healing is a partnership, not a performance.

Healing Practice: The Body Reconciliation Letter

Write a letter to the part of your body you feel has "betrayed" you. You can direct it to your womb, heart, immune system, joints, skin—wherever the pain or rupture occurred.

Include these elements:

- Acknowledgment of the pain
- Expression of how the experience shaped you
- Willingness to hear the body's side of the story
- A statement of reconciliation or openness to rebuild trust

This can be emotional. Go slowly. You don't need to rush forgiveness. Let the self-honesty be enough.

_____

_____

_____

_____

_____

_____

_____

_____

_____

_____

_____

_____

⊚ *Embodiment Practice: Compassionate Touch Ritual*

Choose a part of your body you've been at odds with.

1. Gently place your hands over that area.
2. Close your eyes. Breathe deeply into your hands.
3. Whisper:
4. *"I'm here now. I see you. I'm willing to listen."*
5. Stay with that area for a few minutes. Let any emotions rise without resistance.

Repeat this practice weekly. It's a simple but powerful way to reestablish connection.

📓 *Journal Reflections*

When did I first feel like my body betrayed me? What happened?

_____

_____

_____

_____

_____

What part of me still holds blame? What part of me wants to release it?

_____

_____

_____

_____

_____

What would it feel like to honor my body instead of judge it?

_____

_____

_____

_____

_____

How can I begin to speak to my body with more compassion?

_____

_____

_____

_____

_____

Moving Forward Together

Healing doesn't mean pretending everything is okay. It means making space for all of it—the disappointment, the sorrow, the confusion—and still choosing to show up.

Still choosing to ask:

- What does my body need from me now?
- How can I honor her—not for what she does, but for all she's endured?

You and your body may not always agree, but you're in this together. Every step. Every breath. Every moment.

Let this be the chapter where you shift from blame to bonding. Not because it erases the pain, but because it allows something else to grow in its place: *understanding*.

Your body didn't betray you. She's been surviving with you, the best way she knew how.

And now, perhaps ... *she's ready to heal.*

So are you.

Chapter 11: Reclaiming Inner Respect

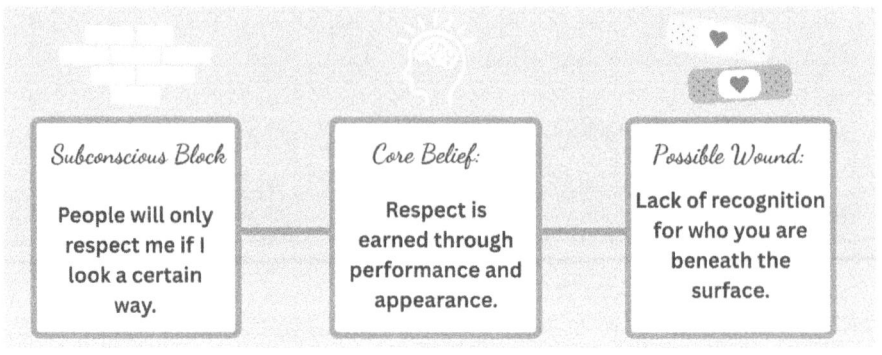

Subconscious Block	*Core Belief:*	*Possible Wound:*
People will only respect me if I look a certain way.	Respect is earned through performance and appearance.	Lack of recognition for who you are beneath the surface.

Layla came to me after years of high-level professional success, but privately, she felt like an imposter in her own skin.

"I know this sounds superficial," she confessed during our first session, "but I don't think people take me seriously unless I'm polished, thin, and flawless. If I let myself be seen as I am ... I'm afraid I'll lose their respect."

Layla had built a life that looked powerful on paper—she ran a six-figure coaching business, spoke on stages, and had a strong online presence. But behind the scenes, she was constantly managing her image. What to wear. What to post. How to look "put together" even when she was grieving, bloated, or burnt out.

Her self-worth was entangled with her presentation. And her confidence was conditional on how closely she could mimic society's idea of "credible."

When we started working together, I gently asked, "Where did you learn that people only respect you if you look a certain way?"

She paused, tears rising. "Everywhere," she said. "Home, school, work, social media—everywhere."

The Unspoken Rule of Worth

This subconscious belief—*that appearance equals respect*—is baked into our culture.

We're taught that "professional" has a look. That success comes with a dress size. That credibility is easier to access if you conform to a particular mold. That "looking the part" is just as important as doing the work.

For empaths, this often results in chronic overcompensation. We try to outperform our insecurities with achievement. We micromanage our bodies, style, and energy to avoid criticism. And we tie our sense of being "enough" to how well we present, not how deeply we live our truth.

Layla's Backstory

Layla's upbringing reinforced this message early on. Her mother was image-conscious and perfection-driven. Her father—a high-profile lawyer—often said things like, "People don't take messy women seriously." It wasn't cruelty. It was conditioning. And it shaped how Layla learned to navigate the world.

She remembered being fifteen and overhearing her mom say to a friend, "Layla's smart, but she'd be unstoppable if she just lost a little weight."

It stuck like glue. So, she worked hard—harder than anyone. She won awards, climbed ladders, became an expert. But underneath the success was a silent rule: *If I don't look the part, I lose the power.*

Cracks in the Illusion

The truth was, Layla was exhausted.

She spent hours prepping for photoshoots. Changed outfits three times before Zoom calls. Avoided social gatherings if she didn't feel "fit enough." She couldn't remember the last time she felt relaxed in her body, especially in front of others.

But what made her reach out was a moment of breakdown in her own coaching program.

A client looked at her through teary eyes and said, "I love how real you are. I feel like I can breathe around you."

It cracked something open. *Real?* Layla hadn't been real in a long time. She'd been strategic. Safe. Respectable.

And deep down, she was craving something else entirely: *authenticity*.

The Shift to Inner Respect

In our healing sessions, Layla began untangling the pattern of equating appearance with power.

I invited her to consider:

> "What if your soul carries a frequency that commands respect, no matter what you look like?"

We explored how her gifts—intuition, presence, empathy, truth—held far more resonance than her wardrobe or waistline ever could. We practiced embodiment rituals to ground her energy in her worth—not just mentally, but viscerally.

She stopped asking, *"Do I look the part?"* and started asking, *"Am I standing in my truth?"*

Her posture changed. Her voice softened. And her leadership expanded—not in image, but in impact.

Reclaiming Respect from Within

True respect doesn't start with others; it starts with how we relate to ourselves.

When we respect our boundaries, our bodies, our voices, and our energy, we teach the world how to meet us.

Layla didn't quit speaking or stop showing up professionally, but she started doing it on her terms. With fuller breath. With clothes that felt like her. With space for softness, not just strength.

And the best part? Her clients respected her more. Because they felt her alignment.

She said, "It turns out people didn't respect me because I looked polished. They respected me because I was present."

💜 *Healing Affirmation*

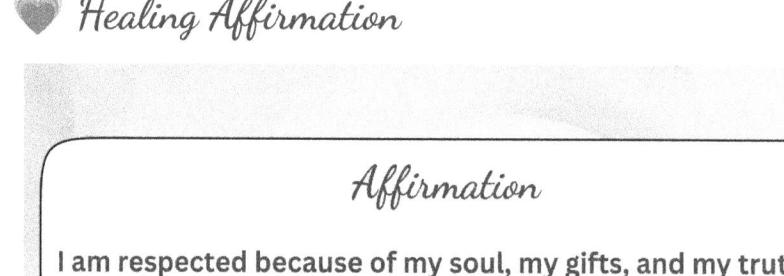

Affirmation

I am respected because of my soul, my gifts, and my truth.

Repeat this anytime you feel the need to overperform or mask yourself for approval. Let it bring you back to center.

✢ *Healing Practice: "Am I Performing or Present?"*

Before a meeting, post, or event, take 60 seconds to ask:

- "Am I showing up to be *respected* or *received*?"
- "What would shift if I led with presence instead of presentation?"

Then place a hand on your heart, take three grounding breaths, and speak this aloud:

"I am enough as I am. I carry my power within me."

Let this become your energetic anchor.

◎ *Embodiment Practice: The Power Posture Ritual*

This daily practice helps embody dignity from within:

1. Stand in front of a mirror with feet hip-width apart.
2. Soften your shoulders. Ground through your feet.
3. Place one hand on your heart and one on your solar plexus.
4. Speak:
5. *"I stand in my truth. I embody respect."*
6. Hold your gaze for 30 seconds. Let your body memorize this feeling.

Repeat daily for 7 days and note any shifts in how you show up.

📓 *Journal Reflections*

What messages did I receive growing up about appearance and respect?

_____

_____

_____

_____

_____

When have I performed for approval, and how did it affect my self-respect?

_____

_____

_____

_____

_____

What qualities do I truly admire in others that have nothing to do with appearance?

_____

_____

_____

_____

_____

What parts of myself am I ready to honor more deeply?

_____

_____

_____

_____

_____

An Invitation to Redefine Respect

Respect isn't a dress code. It's a frequency.

And you don't have to trade your softness, sensitivity, or authenticity to be seen as powerful. In fact, those qualities are what make your leadership *magnetic*.

Let this be the chapter where you stop seeking respect by changing how you look and start embodying it by honoring who you are.

You were never meant to shrink, polish, or perform your way to power.

You were meant to *become the embodiment* of your deepest truth.

And that, more than anything, is what commands the world's attention.

Part III: Stepping into Worthiness

Chapter 12: Taking Up Space

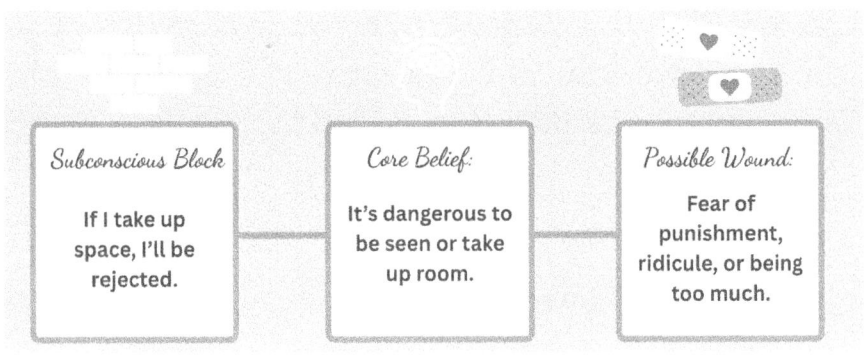

Subconscious Block	Core Belief:	Possible Wound:
If I take up space, I'll be rejected.	It's dangerous to be seen or take up room.	Fear of punishment, ridicule, or being too much.

During a live workshop, a woman named Elena asked to speak. Her voice shook as she held the mic.

"I've spent most of my life trying to disappear," she said. "Not physically, necessarily, but emotionally. Energetically. I've learned how to be invisible, agreeable, and small because ... it didn't feel safe to take up space."

A long silence followed. And then tears. Not just from Elena, but from others who deeply understood her words.

Taking up space sounds like a simple act. But for many empaths, survivors, and sensitive souls, it carries layers of fear. Because once, long ago, showing up fully *wasn't* safe.

The Childhood of Shrinking

Elena's story, like many, began in childhood. She grew up in a home where her presence was tolerated, not celebrated. If she cried too loudly, she was scolded. If she shared an idea, she was interrupted. If she expressed herself too boldly, she was told to tone it down.

Eventually, her nervous system learned:

- *Loud = unsafe*
- *Visible = vulnerable*
- *Authenticity = rejection*

So, she adapted. She made herself likable. Modest. Quiet. Careful. And she stayed that way into adulthood, even when her soul longed for more.

"I have dreams," she told me during our one-on-one work. "But every time I think about stepping forward—starting that business, leading that group—I freeze. I hear a voice saying: *Who do you think you are?*"

This wasn't ego. It was protection. The little girl inside her was still trying to stay safe in the only way she knew how: by staying small.

The Pain of Being Too Much

Many of the clients I've worked with over the years carry a similar scar.

Some were told they were "too sensitive," "too emotional," "too dramatic," or "too intense." Others had moments of visibility—maybe as children, artists, or dreamers—where they were mocked, punished, or dismissed.

So, they shrank. And that shrinking became habitual.

Even when their grown-up self had ideas, gifts, or truths to share, the inner child still whispered, *Better to stay invisible than risk being shamed again.*

Reframing the Fear of Rejection

In one session, I asked Elena:

> "What if taking up space is actually an act of safety now, not danger?"

She paused. "It doesn't feel that way yet," she said honestly. "But I want it to."

That "wanting" was everything. The willingness to rewrite the story. To make a new agreement with her nervous system.

Together, we created rituals of presence. Elena began standing taller, even when no one was watching. She practiced using her voice in safe spaces. She wore clothes that expressed her soul, not just her safety. She made space for herself at the table—literally and metaphorically.

And slowly, her nervous system started catching up to her desire.

The Breakthrough

One day, Elena spoke at a women's gathering. She stood, voice steady, eyes bright, and said:

> "I'm practicing taking up space, and it's not because I'm fearless. It's because I'm done abandoning myself."

She received a standing ovation.

But even more meaningful than that applause? Her own sense of grounded pride.

> "I didn't shrink," she told me later. "I stayed in the room as my full self. And it felt like … coming home."

 ## Healing Affirmation

Affirmation

**It is safe to take up space.
I am worthy of being seen and celebrated.**

Speak this aloud in the mirror. Write it on sticky notes. Say it when you feel your light is starting to dim.

Let these words begin to rewrite your inner narrative.

Healing Practice: The "Expand and Exhale" Ritual

Each morning, before starting your day:

1. Stand with your arms wide open, feet rooted.

2. Inhale deeply and say: "I allow myself to *expand*."

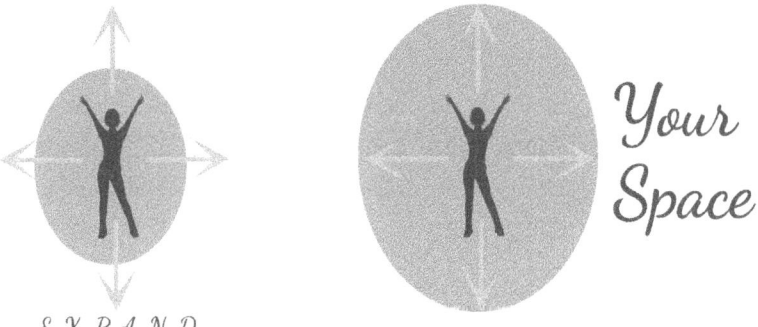

E-X-P-A-N-D

3. Exhale fully and say: "I am safe to be *seen*."

4. Repeat 3 times, feeling your body stretch beyond old limitations.

This daily act of claiming space rewires your subconscious from withdrawal to presence.

◎ *Embodiment Practice: Visibility Journal*

For the next 7 days, answer the following in your journal:

- Where did I allow myself to be *seen* today, even a little?
- What felt scary? What felt empowering?
- What part of me is ready to take up more space tomorrow?

Visibility is about authentic presence. Track your journey *with compassion.*

Did I Let Myself Be Seen Today?

📓 *Journal Reflections*

When did I first learn that it wasn't safe to be fully expressed or visible?

_____

_____

_____

_____

_____

Who or what taught me that taking up space = rejection?

_____

_____

_____

_____

What does taking up space mean to me now?

_____

_____

_____

_____

Where am I ready to stop shrinking?

_____

_____

_____

_____

_____

You Belong in the Room

You don't have to wait to be perfect, healed, or "ready" to show up fully.

You don't have to earn the right to exist boldly, speak clearly, or live loudly.

You belong in the room, in the photo, in the spotlight, in the story.

Let this chapter be the one where you stop making yourself smaller to make others comfortable.

Let it be the moment you breathe deeper, stand taller, and take your seat at the table of your life.

You taking up space is not a threat.

It's a blessing.

It's a reclamation.

It's the return of your full self.

Chapter 13: Releasing Inherited Shame

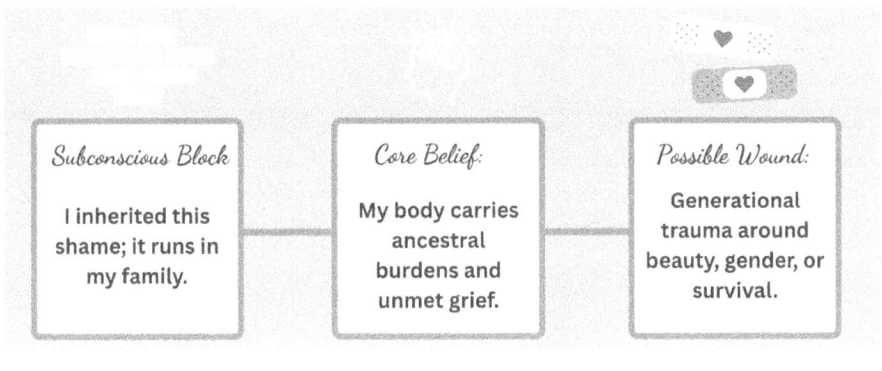

Subconscious Block	Core Belief:	Possible Wound:
I inherited this shame; it runs in my family.	My body carries ancestral burdens and unmet grief.	Generational trauma around beauty, gender, or survival.

When Alina joined my online course, she wasn't expecting ancestral work.

"I came here for body image healing," she said with a soft smile during a breakout room share. "But the more I dig into this, the more I realize … this shame? It's not all mine."

She talked about how women in her family carried a silent legacy of self-denial. Her mother had been raised by a grandmother who never smiled in photos, who never spoke kindly about her body, who believed beauty was both a duty and a burden. "It's like this unspoken rule got passed down," Alina said, "that you should always be improving yourself, but never think too highly of yourself."

Even in moments when Alina *wanted* to feel confident or beautiful, guilt would rise. "It feels like if I love myself too much, I'm betraying where I come from."

Her body held a grief that wasn't just hers—it was ancestral.

The Weight We Carry That isn't Ours

Inherited shame is often invisible, but it shows up in deeply physical ways:

- Tension in the shoulders, jaw, or hips
- Difficulty feeling safe in softness or rest
- Self-sabotage when things start to go well
- A deep inner voice saying, *"Who do you think you are?"*

This isn't always from your lifetime.

Sometimes, we carry the emotional residue of our bloodline, especially when our ancestors weren't allowed or able to process their own pain.

Science now confirms what ancient traditions have always known: trauma can be passed through DNA. So can unprocessed grief, internalized oppression, and body shame.

Where the Shame Begins

Alina's story, like many others, traces back through generations of women who weren't given permission to rest, to express, to expand, or to be seen as sacred in their full-bodied truth.

Her grandmother grew up during wartime scarcity. Her mother, in post-war conservatism. They lived through conditions where survival often meant compliance, invisibility, and silence.

So, when Alina began doing this work—eating intuitively, dressing with confidence, speaking kindly to her reflection—something in her body resisted.

Not because it was wrong.

But because it was *new*, and new often feels threatening to old patterns.

The Legacy of Survival Over Self-Worth

I shared with Alina something I've witnessed with many empathic clients:

> *What feels like resistance is sometimes just your body holding ancestral programming, passed down to keep your lineage safe.*

For generations, your ancestors may have had to suppress their radiance to survive. And now, as you reclaim your voice, your beauty, your worth, old fears may arise.

But that doesn't mean you're wrong.

It means you're the one your lineage has been waiting for.

Alina's Turning Point

Through our work together, Alina began gently acknowledging this inherited weight—not with blame, but with reverence.

We created space for her to honor her matriarchal line while also choosing a new path.

In one powerful ritual, she placed her hands over her heart and womb and said:

> *"I love you. I honor what you endured. And I now choose to release what no longer serves me. I am free to thrive."*

She wept. Not just for herself, but for the women who never got to feel what she was learning to embody.

That was her breakthrough—when she realized self-love wasn't rebellion but reclamation.

 ## Healing Affirmation

Affirmation

**I lovingly release inherited shame.
I honor my lineage and choose healing.**

Speak this slowly, perhaps during a quiet moment or while holding a photo of a loved one. Feel it ripple backward and forward across your lineage.

Healing Practice: Ancestral Release Ritual

You can do this with a candle, a piece of paper, and a quiet moment.

1. Light a candle to represent your family line.
2. Write down beliefs or body image messages you know (or sense) have been passed down.
3. Examples:
   - "My body must be small to be safe."
   - "Beauty is earned, not natural."
   - "Don't be too visible."
4. Read them aloud.
5. Then speak:
6. "I honor the survival behind these beliefs. I release the pain they carried.
7. I choose to be the one who heals forward."
8. Burn or tear the paper, and blow out the candle with gratitude.

Repeat anytime you feel held back by something that doesn't feel like yours.

⊚ Embodiment Practice: Healing the Line

This practice honors your body as a bridge between generations.

1. Lie down or sit with your spine supported.
2. Place one hand on your heart and one on your womb or belly.
3. Breathe into your lower hand and say:
4. "I honor those who came before."
5. Breathe into your upper hand and say:
6. "I choose a new way forward."
7. Rest there, letting your body feel the union of past and future, both held within you.

📓 Journal Reflections

What body beliefs or shame stories might I have inherited from my family?

_____

_____

_____

_____

_____

How did my parents, grandparents, or guardians speak about their own bodies?

_____

_____

_____

_____

_____

What am I ready to release—not out of rejection, but as an act of healing?

_____

_____

_____

_____

_____

What new beliefs do I want to pass forward into my future and the collective field?

_____

_____

_____

You are the Healer of the Line

You are *not here to carry the weight* of all who came before you.

You are here to witness it, bless it, and choose what moves forward through you.

Healing inherited shame doesn't mean you reject your family. It means you honor them by doing what they couldn't. You create new neural pathways—new emotional blueprints—for those who come next.

Let this be the chapter where you stop mistaking heaviness for heritage.

You are not here to shrink like those who had no choice.

You are here to rise.

Chapter 14: Redefining Beauty on Your Own Terms

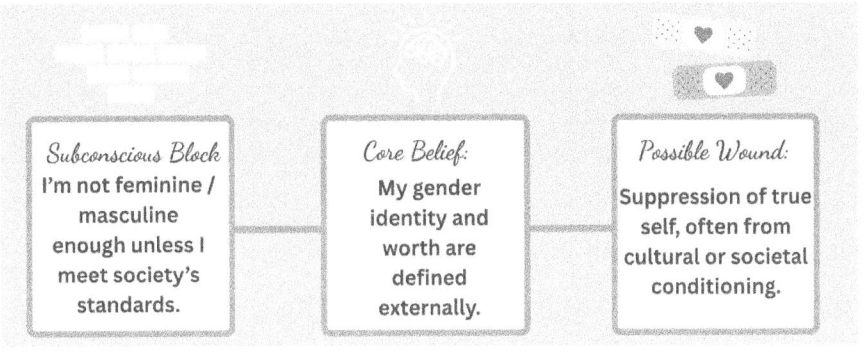

Subconscious Block	Core Belief:	Possible Wound:
I'm not feminine / masculine enough unless I meet society's standards.	My gender identity and worth are defined externally.	Suppression of true self, often from cultural or societal conditioning.

When Kerry joined my *Embodiment Program*, she carried years of tightly held tension beneath her polished surface.

"I've always been driven, decisive, and grounded in strategy over sentiment," she said during our first call. "In my career, those traits were rewarded. But in my personal life, I was told I was too much. Too assertive. Too masculine. I've tried softening myself, being more 'feminine,' but it never felt like me." She paused, eyes searching, then added with quiet vulnerability, "Sometimes, I wonder if I missed the mark on womanhood entirely."

Kerry's struggle wasn't about fitting into gender roles—it was about reclaiming her wholeness.

Beneath her words lived years of conditioning that taught her to succeed by suppressing softness. She carried shame for not fitting the mold of gentle, accommodating femininity. Shame for being ambitious in rooms where women were expected to defer. Shame for trusting logic when she was told she should lead with emotion.

And Kerry is not alone.

I've worked with countless women who have shaped themselves to survive in male-dominated systems—adopting masculine traits to gain credibility, then feeling disconnected from their deeper, more intuitive nature.

This chapter is for every woman who has questioned her worth for being too strong, too bold, too directive … or not soft enough, emotional enough, or pleasing enough.

You are not broken.

You are whole.

And your sacred expression—no matter how it weaves feminine and masculine energies—is worthy of being honored.

This chapter is for those who've ever felt like their truth was too much, too different, or not enough to belong.

And your sacred expression—whatever blend of energies it holds—is worthy of being honored.

When Identity Becomes a Performance

Kerry grew up in a culture where girls were taught to be likable, accommodating, and pretty, but she quickly learned that those qualities didn't get her far in the boardroom.

Early in her career, she started wearing darker suits, speaking in a lower register, and curbing her warmth in meetings. "If I smiled too much, they didn't take me seriously," she told me. "So I became sharper. More direct. I built walls around myself to protect the part of me that still craved tenderness."

But the more she performed, the more distant she felt—not just from others, but from herself.

"I've mastered how to command a room," she said. "But sometimes I don't know how to let someone into my heart. It's like I've trained myself out of softness … and now I don't know how to get it back."

So many women know this feeling.

The Wound of Gender Conditioning

Whether we were raised as girls, boys, or otherwise, most of us were taught a script about how to "be" based on gender:

Women should be nurturing, slim, agreeable—but not "too much."

Men should be strong, stoic, decisive—but not "too soft."

And anyone outside that binary often feels invisible or invalidated.

These messages aren't just limiting—they're wounding. They cut us off from the fullness of our humanity, our expression, and our embodied truth.

When we internalize these ideals, we don't just question how we look. We begin to question how we *are*.

Redefining Beauty from the Inside Out

Kerry's healing began when I invited her to connect with the essence of her strength—not what it looked like externally, but how it felt inside her body.

She closed her eyes and whispered, "It feels like clarity. Like holding the container so others feel safe to unravel. It's direct, but it's grounded in love. It's fierce *and* feminine."

It was powerful. And true.

That moment marked the beginning of Kerry's reclamation—not into a version of herself that fit someone else's idea of womanhood, but into the integrated, soulful leader she was always meant to be.

She didn't need to soften for the world. She needed to *unmask*, to remember who she was before the world told her who she had to become.

💜 *Healing Affirmation*

Affirmation

My expression of femininity, masculinity, or androgyny is uniquely beautiful and valid.

You are the only one who gets to define what your identity looks and feels like.

Say this affirmation aloud with a hand on your heart or your solar plexus. Let your body remember its right to simply be.

Healing Practice: "My Truth, My Terms" Ritual

1. Light a candle or sit quietly in a space that feels safe.
2. Write down all the ways you've tried to fit into gender expectations:
   - How you dress
   - How you speak
   - How you show emotion
   - What you hide
3. Cross out anything that no longer feels true.
4. Then write your own declaration:

5. *"I define my beauty and power on my own terms.*

6. I am valid in how I move, feel, love, and express."

Read this aloud—often—until it becomes a lived truth.

◉ *Embodiment Practice: Gender Energy Integration*

This practice helps you connect to your wholeness beyond binary concepts.

1. Sit comfortably. Close your eyes.
2. Place one hand on your heart (feminine energy center).
3. Place the other on your pelvis (your lower creative center).
4. Breathe into both hands and say:
5. *"All expressions of me are sacred."*
6. Allow yourself to sway, hum, or move if it feels good. Let your body speak.

Repeat whenever you feel disconnected or constricted by roles.

 *Journal Reflections*

What messages did I receive about what femininity, masculinity, or gender "should" look like?

_____

_____

_____

_____

_____

When have I dimmed, denied, or distorted parts of myself to be accepted?

_____

_____

_____

_____

_____

What does *my* unique expression of gender or identity feel like in my body?

_____

_____

_____

_____

_____

How can I create more space to show up as my whole self?

_____

_____

_____

_____

_____

Who You Are is Enough

You don't have to perform womanhood. You don't have to prove manhood. You don't have to conform to societal expectations or cultural norms. You don't have to explain or justify your gender expression to anyone.

You are enough.

You don't have to shave, shape, squeeze, harden, shrink, or exaggerate your being to belong. You already belong.

Let this chapter be your declaration.

No more hiding in plain sight.

No more muting your truth to match someone else's template.

No more waiting to feel valid.

I invite you to take up space in your softness, your strength, your curves, your lines, your fluidity.

You are a living work of art.

And art never apologizes for its expression.

Chapter 15: Honoring the Power of Softness

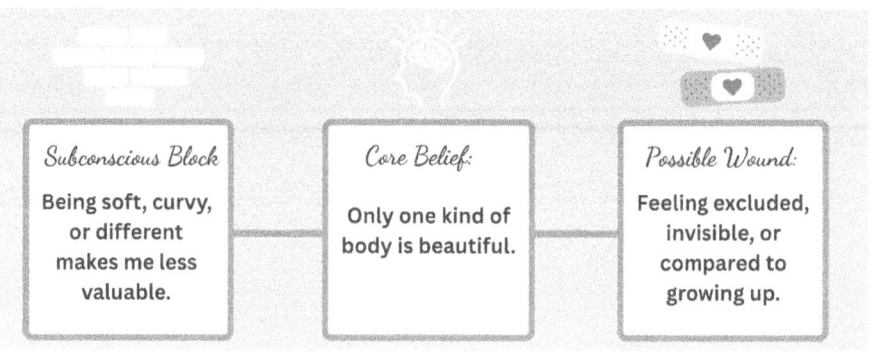

Subconscious Block	Core Belief:	Possible Wound:
Being soft, curvy, or different makes me less valuable.	Only one kind of body is beautiful.	Feeling excluded, invisible, or compared to growing up.

Shayla first came into one of my group programs because she was tired of hating her reflection.

"I've done a lot of healing work," she said, "but when I look in the mirror, all I see is what I *don't* look like. I've always been curvy, and no matter how much I accomplish, I still feel like my softness makes me invisible in this world." She had tears in her eyes. "I don't want to spend another year trying to take up less space. But I don't know how to feel beautiful the way that I am."

Shayla's words echoed something I've heard from so many women: the belief that if we're not toned, lean, or sculpted like the magazine cover ideal, we are somehow less—less seen, less chosen, less powerful.

This subconscious block doesn't just impact body image—it erodes self-worth. It tells us that to be accepted, we must be different from how we naturally are. It continually whispers in our ear, "softness is a weakness," "our curves are flaws," and "difference equals disapproval."

Stop listening to the whispers and rewrite your story.

When the World Rewards Sameness

Shayla was praised for her intellect, her kindness, her leadership, but rarely for her body. Growing up, her friends were smaller, more traditionally "modelesque," and got attention in ways she never did. Boys called her "cute," but never "hot." Even the compliments she received felt lukewarm, like consolation prizes.

She told me, "I always felt like the 'supportive friend.' The person people liked *despite* how I looked. So I stopped trying to be seen that way."

So she hid—not overtly, but in subtle, daily ways:

- Wearing black instead of bold colors
- Turning her body sideways in photos
- Laughing off compliments
- Believing beauty just wasn't "her lane"

Even when she found self-love in other areas, this wound stayed embedded in her body. And she was ready—finally—to heal it.

Why This Block Runs So Deep

We live in a culture that pushes a narrow, often unattainable beauty ideal. If your body doesn't fit the dominant mold—whether that's based on size, race, ability, age, or shape—you can internalize the idea that your value is conditional.

And for empaths, this message hits especially hard.

Because you don't just hear it—you *feel* it. The comments. The comparisons. The subtle ways people react to different bodies. It's like you absorb the shame before it's even spoken.

But here's what I shared with Shayla and what I offer to you now:

> *Your softness is not a liability. It's a language. It speaks of power, compassion, creativity, and depth. Softness is sacred.*

Shayla's Turning Point

In one session, we did an embodiment practice where she laid one hand over her heart and the other on her belly. I invited her to simply breathe—no fixing, no analyzing—just to feel the natural rhythm of her body.

After a few moments, she whispered, "I've never touched my belly like this with kindness before."

That moment cracked something open.

She began to explore what her body *wanted* to wear, not what would "slim" her. She danced in her kitchen again. She showed up in brighter colors. She stopped apologizing for the space she took up—in her body and in her brilliance.

Weeks later, Shayla said:

> "I realized that I've been trying to be smaller to make others comfortable. But now? I want to be fully expressed, even if it makes people look twice."

And they did—not because she changed her body, but because she stopped hiding in it.

🩶 *Healing Affirmation*

> ## *Affirmation*
>
> **Softness is strength.**
> **My body is a beautiful expession of my spirit.**

Say this with hands on your curves, your softness, your fullness. Let it soak into the places that once felt like too much.

Healing Practice: Mirror Blessing for Softness

Once a week, create space to gently return to the softness within you—through slow movement and conscious breath.

Set the space:

Dim the lights, light a candle, and play soft instrumental or nature-based music.

Begin with breath:

Place one hand on your heart and one on your womb (or lower belly).

Inhale slowly through your nose, hold your breath, and then exhale through your mouth in equal counts.

Repeat this for 3-5 minutes, letting your body unwind.

Move intuitively:

Let your body sway, stretch, or spiral without needing it to look a certain way.

Imagine you're moving through honey. Let each gesture be slow, sensual, sacred.

Feel your hips, your shoulders, your chest. Let them soften.

Whisper affirmations as you move:

"I am allowed to be soft and strong."

"My softness is sacred, not weakness."

"I trust the wisdom of my body."

Close with stillness:

Sit or lie down and place both hands over your heart.

Feel the pulse of life within you.

Say aloud:

"I welcome softness. I welcome grace. I welcome me."

Tears, tingles, and deep breaths are all welcome. Let this be a coming home.

⊚ *Embodiment Practice: Curve Celebration Movement*

Create a playlist that makes you feel sensual, alive, and powerful. And if you haven't yet heard my uplifting and empowering music, check my albums out at TiffanysHappySongs.com for your playlist ideas.

Then:

1. Stand tall. Place your hands on your hips, waist, or any place you want to celebrate.
2. Let your body move freely—not to burn calories, but to express freedom.
3. With each movement, repeat:
4. "*I take* up space with pride. *I dance* with my curves. *I am* art in motion."

Let it be messy, imperfect, and deliciously yours.

📔 Journal Reflections

What parts of my body have I felt pressure to change in order to feel valuable?

_____

_____

_____

_____

_____

When did I first learn that softness or curves made me less desirable?

_____

_____

_____

_____

_____

How would I show up differently if I believed my natural shape was already beautiful?

_____

_____

_____

_____

_____

What stories am I ready to retire, and what truths am I ready to live?

_____

_____

_____

Celebrating the Body You Came In

You don't have to earn the right to feel beautiful.

You don't have to tone down, tighten up, or tuck in your softness to be seen as sacred.

Let this be the chapter where you stop hiding behind black clothes and self-deprecating jokes.

Let it be the moment you wear what you want, not what minimizes you.

Let it be the shift from shrinking to shining.

There is no "wrong" way to have a body.

There is only the way *you* embody your spirit.

And that—soft, curvy, angular, freckled, fierce—is divine.

Chapter 16: Loving Yourself Through Every Season

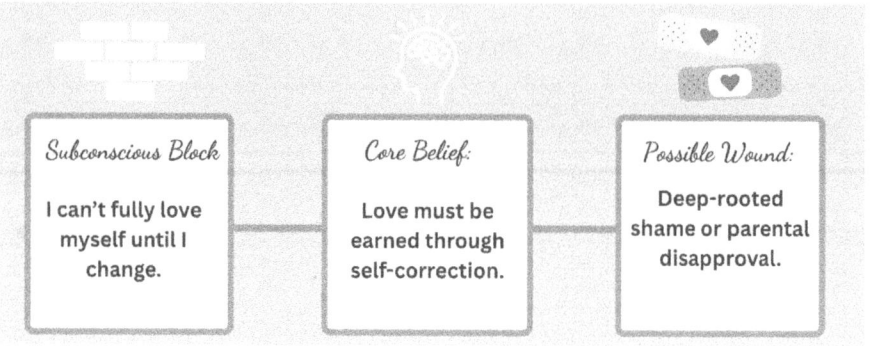

Subconscious Block	Core Belief:	Possible Wound:
I can't fully love myself until I change.	Love must be earned through self-correction.	Deep-rooted shame or parental disapproval.

Sierra reached out to me after following my work for over a year.

She wrote, "I'm not new to healing. I've done therapy, coaching, and inner child work. But there's still this voice inside me that says, *You can't relax into love until you've earned it.* I keep waiting to arrive at some better version of me before I allow myself to rest or feel proud."

When we spoke, she shared a sentiment that so many carry quietly:

> "I'll love myself once I'm more consistent. Once I stop self-sabotaging. Once I actually stick to the goals I set. Right now … I feel like a walking contradiction."

Her voice was layered with insight and exhaustion.

Sierra didn't hate herself, but she didn't *trust* herself either. She saw every flaw as proof that she hadn't yet "earned" the right to feel lovable.

This belief is one of the most common and corrosive:

That we must earn love through improvement.

That acceptance must be postponed until perfection.

Where This Story Begins

Sierra's childhood was achievement-focused. She was praised when she won awards, when she looked polished, when she didn't cry. But when she gained weight, when she was emotional, when she made mistakes, she was met with silence or sharp correction.

Over time, she equated self-love with productivity. Discipline. Fixing.

And so, even as an adult doing deep inner work, there remained an internalized rule: *I must first become "better" before I am worthy of my own tenderness.*

It's a belief that sneaks in quietly but stays rooted.

It often sounds like:

- "Once I'm more healed …"
- "When I lose the weight …"

- "After I stop procrastinating ..."
- "If I just work harder ..."

But love delayed becomes love denied.

Breaking the Cycle of Conditional Love

In one of our sessions, I asked Sierra to visualize herself at her lowest point—disappointed, off track, emotionally messy. Then I invited her to place her hand on her heart and say:

"Even now, I love you."

She froze. "I can't. It feels fake."

But she tried again. Softer. Slower.

Tears came almost immediately.

Not because it was wrong—but because it was *new.*

Her system had never learned to associate mistakes or messiness with love. She had only ever received love when she stood out and was impressive.

That moment began a new practice: *loving herself through every season, not just the harvest.*

What Self-Love Really Means

Self-love isn't a reward. It's a relationship.

It's not just bubble baths and affirmations—it's how you treat yourself when you mess up. When you binge. When you cancel the workout. When you ghost your coach. When your inner critic gets loud.

Loving yourself means showing up with compassion, not conditions.

It's saying:

> "Even when I fall short, I am still worthy of care."
> "Even when I don't follow through, I am still allowed to rest."
> "Even when I'm scared, stuck, or slow, I am enough."

Sierra's Transformation

Over time, Sierra began to release the belief that her love had to be *earned.*

She created new rituals:

- Saying "I love you" to herself after hard days, not just successful ones
- Speaking to her body kindly even when she felt bloated
- Celebrating follow-through *and* compassion when she didn't follow through

She didn't become "perfect." She became *present.*

And one day, she messaged me this:

> "I've been consistent with self-love, even when I wasn't consistent with my habits. For the first time, I'm not afraid of falling off track. Because I know I'll meet myself with grace."

That's what real growth looks like.

💜 *Healing Affirmation*

Affirmation

I love myself now AND in every shape I've ever been.

Say this aloud. Write it on your bathroom mirror. Let it become a new truth in your body.

Healing Practice: Love Letter to Your In-Between Self

1. Write a letter to the version of you who feels unfinished, behind, or messy.

2. Begin with:

3. "I see you, and I love you. Even now."

4. Include all the things you admire about this version, not just where you're going.

5. End with:

6. "You are not a project. You are a person. And *I choose to love you as you are.*"

Reread this whenever you feel tempted to postpone your own tenderness.

◎ *Embodiment Practice: Love Through Movement*

1. Put on music that feels gentle and grounding.

2. Place your hands on your body—wherever feels disconnected or criticized.

3. With each breath, whisper, "*I choose to love this part of me.*"

4. Move slowly. No choreography. Just presence.

Let your body receive the message it's been craving: *unconditional acceptance.*

 *Journal Reflections*

What would change if I believed I didn't have to "earn" love or worth?

_____

_____

_____

_____

_____

When have I postponed joy or rest until I improved?

_____

_____

_____

_____

_____

How did my family or culture teach me to associate love with performance?

_____

_____

_____

_____

_____

- What rituals could help me feel loved *now*, not "after"?

You Are Lovable in Every Season

You don't need to wait until you're "healed" to be kind to yourself.

You don't have to be at your most productive, beautiful, or balanced to be worthy of love.

You're not a project.

You're a soul in motion. A spirit in skin. A sacred being who deserves tenderness in every chapter, not just the ones with happy endings.

Let this be the moment you stop waiting to love yourself.

Let this be the chapter where you say:

"I am lovable, even here. Especially here."

Part IV: Releasing People-Pleasing & Fear

Chapter 17: Releasing Responsibility for Others' Opinions

Subconscious Block

I'm responsible for how others feel about my body.

Core Belief:

It's my job to make everyone comfortable.

Possible Wound:

People-pleasing or emotional caretaking at the cost of self.

Tanya sat across from me in a healing circle, her shoulders drawn in, her voice barely above a whisper.

"I know I'm not supposed to care what other people think," she said. "But I do. If someone stares, if someone makes a comment, even if someone praises me, I overanalyze it. I feel like I have to constantly manage the way others *feel about* me and live up to their expectations of how I should look." There was a long pause, and then she added, "It's exhausting. I feel like I'm never allowed to just be in my body, because I'm always in someone else's gaze."

The room went quiet—not because there was nothing to say, but because almost every woman in that circle had felt the same.

The Burden of Managing Perception

Tanya had spent most of her life as the "nice one." The one who smoothed tension, deflected conflict, kept the peace. Her kindness wasn't fake—it was a survival skill. Somewhere along the way, she picked up a silent contract:

> "I'll make sure you're okay with me, even if I'm not okay with myself."

It showed up in every area of her life, and especially around her body.

She'd dress to avoid making others uncomfortable, or avoid wearing things she loves just in case they may "draw attention." If someone complimented her, she'd immediately downplay it. If someone judged her, she'd internalize it as her fault.

Her body was constantly under surveillance—not just from others, but from the inner monitor she had developed to protect herself.

And deep down, she was afraid that if she *didn't* manage others' comfort, she'd lose belonging, respect, or even safety.

Where This Pattern Begins

For so many empaths and highly sensitive souls, people-pleasing doesn't start as vanity. It starts as survival.

Maybe you grew up in a household where your emotions were too big for your family. Maybe you were told to tone it down, be less sensitive, stay quiet. Or maybe you were the one who had to mediate, soothe, or keep everyone else calm.

You learned that being "too much" created tension. So you adapted. You became smaller, safer, easier to digest.

And when it comes to your body, you may have learned to view yourself through the imagined comfort of others.

This belief often sounds like:

- "I don't want to make anyone uncomfortable."
- "If I'm going to be bigger, I have to be extra likable."
- "If I'm too attractive, I'll be resented or objectified."
- "If I dress a certain way, I'm asking for judgment."

But here's the truth I offered Tanya, and what I want to offer you now:

> ***You are not responsible*** *for other people's discomfort with your body.*

You never were.

Tanya's Turning Point

In one of our sessions, Tanya and I practiced a visualization where she stood in the center of a field—grounded, embodied, surrounded by light and healthy energetic boundaries. Around her, images of past experiences floated by: the rude comment from a co-worker, the silence from a date, the backhanded compliment from a relative.

But, this time, instead of shrinking or adjusting, she stood tall.

I asked her to speak to each image, one by one. She said:

"That's not mine."
"That's not mine either."
"And that? Definitely not mine."
I'm a yes to positive, empowering energies.
I'm unavailable for other people's anger, judgment, and criticism.
I have clear YESes and clear NOs.

Tears came. But not from pain. From *release*.

She finally gave herself permission to stop carrying the expectations that never belonged to her.

Be UN-available for Other Peoples' Negative Energies

no

no

yes

yes

yes

yes

no

no

Healthy Energetic Boundary

What Becomes Possible When You Let Go

When you release responsibility for others' perceptions, so much opens up:

- You wear what feels good, not what's safe.
- You speak your truth, even if it makes others squirm.
- You feel free to be joyful, embodied, radiant, without guilt.
- You trust yourself more than anyone else's projections.

And most of all, you start to live for yourself, not the imagined opinions in the room.

Are you ready to empty out other people's energies and expectations of you?

Tanya didn't stop caring about people, but she stopped managing their expectations of her. And, in doing so, she started experiencing her body not as a performance, but as a home.

💜 Healing Affirmation

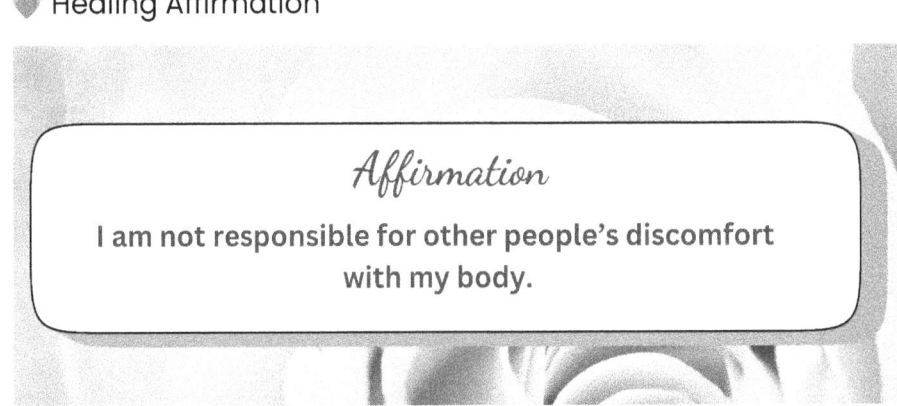

Affirmation

I am not responsible for other people's discomfort with my body.

Say this aloud when you feel the urge to shrink, please, or apologize for your existence. It's not your job to shrink for someone else's comfort.

🌿 Healing Practice: Projection Release Ceremony

1. Write down the comments, looks, or judgments that still linger in your energy.
2. Examples:
   - "You looked better last year."
   - "Are you really wearing *that?*"
   - "You'd be prettier if …"
3. Light a candle. Read each one aloud and say after each:
4. "This is not mine to carry."
5. Tear or burn the paper. Blow out the candle. Feel the weight release.

Do this as many times as needed. Releasing projection is a sacred maintenance of your energy field.

🌀 Embodiment Practice: The "Sacred Sovereignty" Walk

1. Go for a short walk—ideally outside, in nature.
2. As you walk, repeat to yourself with each step:

3. *"I belong to myself."*
4. "I am safe to be seen."
5. "I take up space on my terms."
6. With each step, feel your ownership of your body, your breath, your beauty.

Let it be a practice of reclaiming your presence, unapologetically.

📓 Journal Reflections

When did I start believing I had to manage other people's responses to my body?

_____

_____

_____

_____

_____

What have I done or avoided in the name of "not making others uncomfortable?"

_____

_____

_____

_____

_____

How would I live, dress, move, or show up if I released that responsibility?

_____

_____

_____

_____

_____

What part of me is ready to feel safe in self-ownership?

_____

_____

_____

_____

_____

You Get to Be Free

You are allowed to be desirable, expressive, quiet, loud, curvy, lean, soft, strong, emotional, sensual, sacred.

You do not need to tone down your essence or adjust your shape to be more palatable.

Let this chapter be the one where you let go of their projections.

Let this be the moment you say:

> *"I will not carry what isn't mine. I belong to myself now."*

You are not here to please the crowd.

You are here to live in your body like it's your birthright.

Because it is.

Chapter 18: Stepping into Visibility

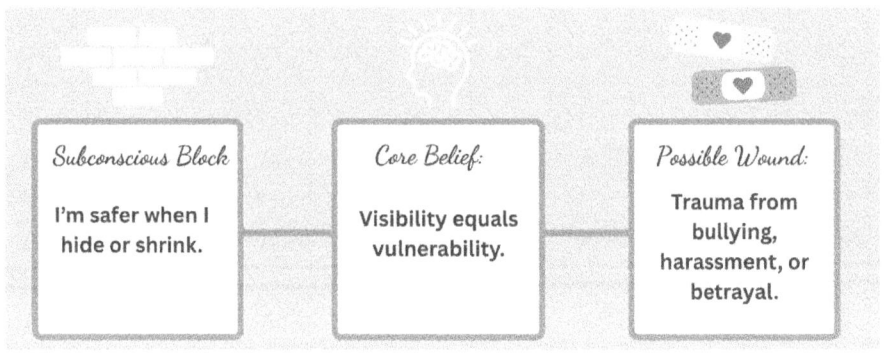

Subconscious Block	Core Belief:	Possible Wound:
I'm safer when I hide or shrink.	Visibility equals vulnerability.	Trauma from bullying, harassment, or betrayal.

At a retreat I led, one woman sat toward the back of the room for the first day and a half. She was quiet, present, and observant. I noticed how often she offered insight in writing exercises but rarely spoke aloud.

On the second evening, during a heart circle, she finally raised her hand. Her name was Renée.

"I want to be seen," she said softly, "but I feel like every time I get close to that, I go into hiding. My nervous system goes into lockdown. It's like I still believe that being seen = being hurt." Her voice cracked as she spoke. "It's just safer to stay small."

You could feel the whole room exhale with recognition.

The Body Remembers

Renée had been bullied as a teen. When her body started changing—curves forming, voice deepening, expression becoming bolder—she was met with unwanted attention, rumors, and shaming. She learned quickly: visibility could be dangerous.

So, she disappeared—not physically, but energetically.

She dimmed her light in photos. She skipped the talent show. She never spoke up, even when she had wisdom to share.

By the time she entered adulthood, the pattern was deeply ingrained. Any time she considered showing more of herself—whether in a relationship, a presentation, or even on social media—her body tensed, her breath shortened, and her mind whispered, *Don't do it. You'll get hurt again.*

The Visibility Wound

Many of us carry a visibility wound, especially those who identify as empaths, sensitives, creatives, or survivors.

Maybe you were criticized and judged.

Maybe someone used your vulnerability against you.

Maybe you were laughed at when you expressed joy.

Maybe your beauty was sexualized before you felt safe in it.

Maybe no one protected you when you needed to be seen in your pain.

And so, your body began to associate being seen with danger.

But here's what I shared with Renée and what I want to offer to you now:

> Being visible is not inherently dangerous. It's the lack of safety around that visibility that created the fear.

The wound wasn't wrong, but the story can be rewritten.

Reclaiming the Right to Be Seen

In our retreat, I guided Renée through a mirror practice. At first, she couldn't meet her own gaze for more than a second. But when we brought in breathwork, grounding, and gentle self-touch, something shifted.

She looked into her eyes and said:

> "I see you. I'm not going to abandon you again."

Tears flowed—not just from grief, but from *relief.*

That was the first time she allowed her body to feel safe in its own visibility.

And in the final circle of the retreat, she spoke first. Boldly. Clearly. With her whole voice.

Why Visibility is Part of Your Healing

Visibility isn't about being loud, extroverted, or performative.

It's about *being present in your body and your truth.* Even when it's quiet. Even when it's vulnerable.

Being visible is how you let yourself be known—not just to the world, but to yourself.

And when you reclaim visibility, you're no longer waiting for external permission to exist. You give that permission to yourself.

💜 Healing Affirmation

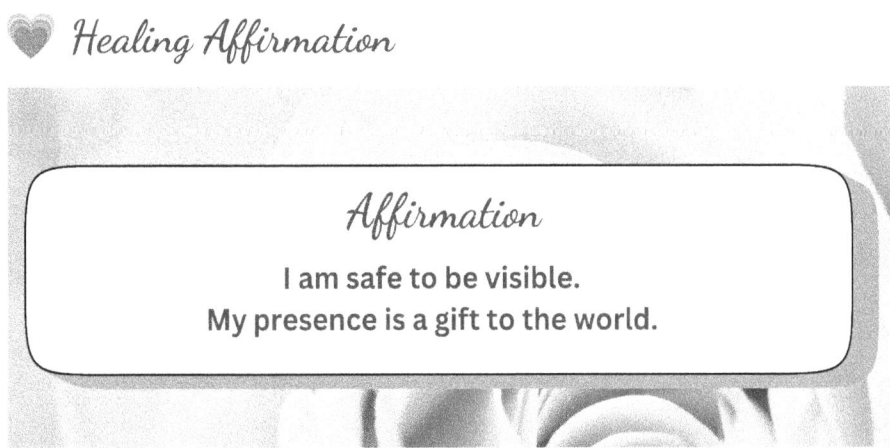

Affirmation

I am safe to be visible.
My presence is a gift to the world.

Place your hand on your throat and heart as you speak this aloud. Let your body begin to believe that being seen can be sacred.

Healing Practice: Sacred Mirror Reclamation

Do this for 3 days in a row to begin building a new relationship with visibility.

1. Stand in front of a mirror. Ground your feet. Breathe.
2. Look into your eyes. Not to critique. Just to *witness.*
3. Say slowly and clearly:
4. *"It is safe to be seen.* I let my light shine."
5. "I am here. I am whole. I am ready."
6. Smile at yourself—not from performance, but from presence.

This may bring up emotion. Let it. It's a sign that your nervous system is recalibrating.

Embodiment Practice: Spotlight Circle

This practice can be done alone or with trusted friends:

1. Stand or sit in a circle space. Imagine a warm spotlight over your body.

2. Place one hand on your solar plexus, the other on your heart.
3. Speak aloud or journal:
   - "Here's one thing I've hidden about myself."
   - "Here's one thing I'm proud of but afraid to share."
   - "Here's what I want to be seen for."
4. Close with:
5. "I allow myself to be fully known and fully safe."

Practice regularly to desensitize fear and invite safety into expression.

📓 Journal Reflections

When did I first associate visibility with fear or pain?

_____

_____

_____

_____

_____

What are the parts of me I've been hiding, and why?

_____

_____

_____

_____

_____

What would change in my life if I trusted that I could be seen and safe?

_____

_____

_____

_____

_____

What do I most long to be witnessed for?

_____

_____

_____

_____

_____

You Deserve to Be Seen

You are not too much.

You are not too loud, too soft, too curvy, too radiant, too expressive.

You are *exactly right* in your full presence.

Let this be the chapter where you stop editing yourself for safety.

Let this be where you stop rehearsing and start revealing.

The world doesn't need your perfection.

It needs your presence.

You are safe now.

You are powerful now.

And you are ready.

Chapter 19: Embracing the Sacredness of the Body

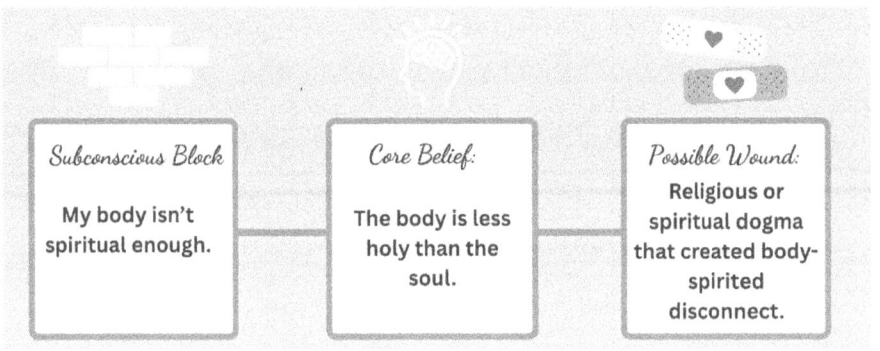

Subconscious Block	Core Belief:	Possible Wound:
My body isn't spiritual enough.	The body is less holy than the soul.	Religious or spiritual dogma that created body-spirited disconnect.

Raisa arrived with a beautiful heart and a quiet struggle.

She was deeply spiritual—devoted to meditation, intuitive practices, and a rich inner life. But when it came to her body, there was a disconnect.

"I know the soul is sacred," she told me during our intake session, "but I still struggle to see my body that way. I've always felt like it's something I have to transcend ... not inhabit." Her voice trembled a little. "I feel connected to angels, but not to my own hips."

That sentence held so much. For Raisa—and for many on a spiritual path—the body had become more of a burden than a blessing. Something she tolerated while seeking divine connection. Something she disciplined, quieted, and occasionally resented.

And underneath it all lived the subconscious belief: *My body is not spiritual.*

The Disconnection Rooted in Dogma

Raisa was raised in a conservative religious environment where the body was spoken about with caution, if at all. Desire was sinful. Beauty was vanity. Physical pleasure was a distraction. Her early teachings didn't offer reverence for the body, only rules and warnings.

So, she ascended. She learned to meditate for hours. She cultivated light. She developed her gifts. But when it came time to be seen, touched, or express physically, she'd shut down.

"I'm more comfortable in other dimensions than I am in my own skin," she told me.

This wasn't a rejection of the body out of vanity. It was spiritual self-protection. And she wasn't alone in it.

When Spirituality Becomes an Escape

In the healing world, it's easy to idolize the upper chakras—intuition, vision, connection to the divine—while ignoring or bypassing the lower ones, which govern embodiment, sensuality, and safety.

But true spiritual integration doesn't float above the body. You are a spiritual being with a body temple, and it's important to occupy it.

Our bodies are not separate from our spiritual path—they *are* the path. Every breath, every heartbeat, every sensation is an invitation into presence, into incarnation.

So, I offered Raisa a reframe:

> "What if your body isn't the opposite of your spirit, but the expression of it?"

That was the beginning of her return.

Reclaiming the Sacred Vessel

In one session, I guided Raisa through a somatic practice, placing her hands over her heart and womb, breathing deeply, and saying:

> "This is my temple. My body is a holy place."

At first, she cried.

"I've spent so long trying to get out of my body," she said. "But I think she's been waiting for me to come home."

That was the moment her healing deepened—not because she fixed her body, but because she *remembered* its sacredness.

 *Healing Affirmation*

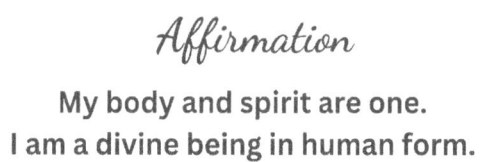

Affirmation

My body and spirit are one.
I am a divine being in human form.

Repeat this aloud. Place a hand on your chest or womb as you say it. Let it echo through your cells like a blessing.

Healing Practice: Sacred Anointing Ritual

This practice honors your body as a spiritual vessel.

1. Choose a natural oil or lotion that feels nourishing.
2. In a quiet space, light a candle and take a few grounding breaths.
3. As you gently massage the oil into different parts of your body, speak blessings aloud:

- o "I honor my feet—they walk my sacred path."
- o "I honor my belly—it carries wisdom and life."
- o "I honor my hands—they offer healing."
4. End by whispering:
5. *"I return home to my sacred self."*

This ritual can be done monthly, weekly, or whenever you feel disconnected from your body.

⊚ *Embodiment Practice: Root to Crown Integration*

Use this practice to harmonize the energy centers of your body:

1. Sit or lie down with one hand on your lower belly and one on your crown.
2. Inhale into the root: *"I am grounded."*
3. Exhale from the crown: "I am guided."
4. Repeat for 5 cycles, visualizing energy flowing from sky to earth, and earth to sky, *through* your body.

Let your spine be the bridge between heaven and earth.

G
R
O
U
N
D

 *Journal Reflections*

What messages have I received that separated my body from my spirituality?

_____

_____

_____

_____

_____

How have I tried to "transcend" rather than befriend my body?

_____

_____

_____

_____

_____

What does it feel like to imagine my body as sacred?

_____

_____

_____

_____

_____

What new relationship do I want to cultivate with my physical self?

_____

_____

_____

_____

_____

Your Body is a Temple, Not a Test

You are not here to float above your form.

You are here to *embody the divine.*

To breathe spirit through skin.

To make love a lived experience, not just a lofty ideal.

Your softness is not a sin.

Your curves are not a curse.

Your hunger is not a flaw.

Your body is not a distraction.

It is *the place where the sacred lives.*

Let this be the chapter where you stop trying to escape and start remembering:

> *You don't have to leave your body to feel God.*
> *You are holy, right here, in this breath, in this form,*
> *in this skin.*

You are not just a soul having a human experience.

You are a soul dancing in a sacred vessel.

Welcome home.

Chapter 20: Redefining Power Through Self-Compassion

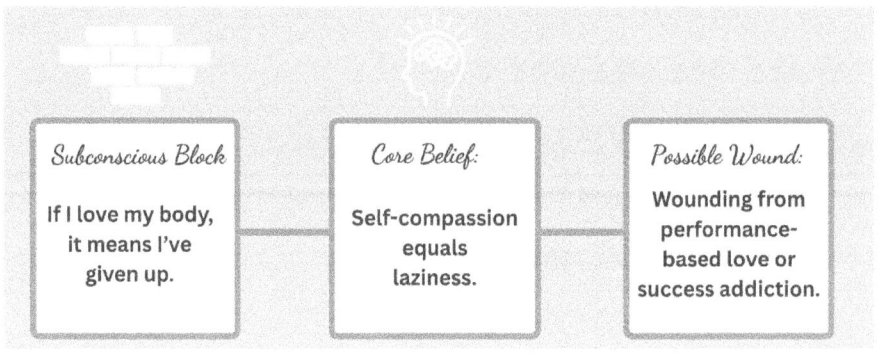

Subconscious Block	Core Belief:	Possible Wound:
If I love my body, it means I've given up.	Self-compassion equals laziness.	Wounding from performance-based love or success addiction.

When Nicole joined my coaching circle, she introduced herself with a familiar tension.

"I'm here because I want to stop the war with my body," she said, "but I'm terrified that if I actually *accept* myself, I'll stop evolving. I'll let myself go. And I won't be motivated to change anything."

Her voice was clear, but there was a quiet heartbreak underneath. The unspoken part: *I don't trust myself to hold love and growth at the same time.*

Nicole, like many high-performing women I've worked with, had internalized a message that loving yourself too soon would make you complacent. That self-compassion was indulgent. That softness would dull her drive.

So, she pushed. She perfected what she could about herself. She shamed herself into striving.

And yet, she was exhausted.

The Shame-Driven Success Trap

Nicole had always been "the achiever." Straight A's. Fit. Focused. Composed. From the outside, her life looked impeccable. But her relationship with her body was entirely conditional.

She told me, "If I skip a workout or eat something 'off plan,' the guilt is immediate. And the voice in my head isn't just disappointed—it's *vicious*."

Her motivation was rooted in fear. If she let go of the hypervigilance, even for a moment, she was sure everything would unravel.

But what she didn't realize was this: shame was not sustainable fuel. And the cost of using it was her peace.

Where This Belief Comes From

Many of us were raised in systems that reward performance and punish rest.

Maybe you were praised when you achieved and criticized when you slowed down. Maybe love was given when you succeeded and withheld when you struggled. Maybe "tough love" was the only kind of love you knew.

So you learned:

- *Be hard on yourself, or you'll fall behind.*
- *Don't celebrate too early—there's more to do.*
- *If you stop pushing, you'll lose your edge.*

But here's what I told Nicole:

> *Self-compassion doesn't mean you've given up. It means you've shifted from fear to faith.*

It's not about becoming less driven. It's about becoming more aligned.

Nicole's Turning Point

One day, we explored what would happen if she *didn't* fix something after "messing up."

I invited her into a radical experiment: to skip the self-punishment cycle after a missed goal. Just one time. To respond with kindness instead of control.

She tried it.

After missing a workout, instead of spiraling into shame, she placed her hands on her heart and said, "It's okay. I'm still worthy of love. I'll move when I'm ready."

She texted me the next day:

> *"That was the most productive day I've had in weeks. I didn't lose motivation—I gained energy. I finally exhaled."*

That's the paradox: self-compassion doesn't slow growth—it *amplifies* it. Because, when your nervous system feels safe, you stop operating from survival and start creating from sovereignty.

 Healing Affirmation

Affirmation
Loving my body is an act of power, not defeat.

Speak this with your spine tall, your hands open, and your heart soft. Let it become a new truth in your tissues.

✦ Healing Practice: Rewriting the Motivation Mantra

1. Reflect on what you currently say to yourself when you don't meet your expectations.
2. Write those thoughts down on paper. Be honest. No censoring.
3. Then rewrite each one through the lens of love.
4. Examples:
   - "You're so lazy." → **"You're allowed to rest."**
   - "You always mess up." → **"Every moment is a new choice."**
   - "No one will love you like this." → **"I love you exactly like this."**

Choose one of your new mantras and speak it daily, especially when old patterns arise.

⊚ Embodiment Practice: Compassionate Core Connection

This practice connects your willpower (core) with your compassion (heart).

1. Sit or stand with a hand over your heart and one over your belly.
2. Breathe deeply into both.
3. Say:

4. "My power and softness work together."
5. "I grow with *grace*. I change with *love*."
6. Stay here for 3-5 minutes, simply noticing what shifts in your body.

Repeat weekly or whenever you feel torn between pushing and pausing.

Journal Reflections

Where did I learn that love must be earned through effort?

_____

_____

_____

_____

_____

What do I fear would happen if I stopped criticizing or pushing myself?

_____

_____

_____

_____

_____

How might self-compassion *increase* my capacity rather than decrease it?

_____

_____

_____

_____

_____

What new definition of strength feels true to me now?

_____

_____

_____

_____

_____

You are Allowed to be Soft and Strong

You don't have to harden to be powerful.

You don't have to punish yourself to demonstrate progress.

You don't have to wait until you "get it together" to treat yourself with respect.

Let this be the chapter where you stop driving your growth with a whip and start guiding it with a hand over your heart.

You are not giving up by loving yourself now.

You are rising, with more truth, more gentleness, more integrity.

Because love isn't the end of transformation.

It's where the *real* transformation begins.

Repeat to yourself: "*I am Soft and Strong!*"

Chapter 21: You are Enough

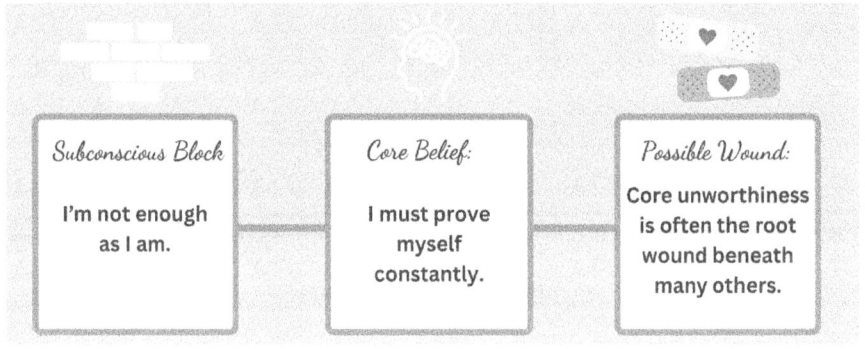

Subconscious Block	Core Belief:	Possible Wound:
I'm not enough as I am.	I must prove myself constantly.	Core unworthiness is often the root wound beneath many others.

When Malia entered my group program, she was successful on the surface—smart, grounded, and deeply intuitive. But when it came to receiving, she shut down.

"I give a lot," she said during our first group call, "but I don't know how to let love in. Compliments, support, even joy—it all makes me uncomfortable. I just … never feel like I've done enough to deserve it." She smiled a little nervously. "Sometimes, I feel like I have to keep achieving or performing, or I'll disappear."

Her words pierced through the virtual circle. So many nodded. Because this is the wound that sits beneath so many others. The ancient, aching question:

Am I enough?

The Root of the Wound

Malia grew up in a home where success was the currency of love. Her parents weren't cruel, but they were conditioned. They celebrated when she brought home straight A's. They applauded when she won awards. But when she simply wanted to *be*, they were distant, distracted.

She learned to associate worth with effort. To equate rest with risk. To believe that love was something to be earned, not received.

And like so many highly sensitive souls, she became exceptional at being needed, but quietly terrified of being *seen*.

The Ways We Chase "Enough"

The "not enough" wound wears many disguises. It might look like:

- Constantly signing up for new trainings or certifications
- Feeling like you need to be "healed" before you're worthy
- Being there for everyone but never asking for help
- Feeling guilt when you rest
- Trying to control your appearance to feel valuable

- Struggling to receive without immediately reciprocating

It's the silent agreement so many of us make:

If I just do more, give more, achieve more … maybe then I'll feel like enough.

But the truth is: no amount of external validation can fill the space where self-belonging is meant to live.

Malia's Turning Point

In one of our sessions, I invited Malia into a reparenting practice—an inner dialogue between her adult self and the younger part of her that still felt unseen.

Eyes closed, hand on her heart, she whispered:

> "You don't have to earn my love anymore. You're already enough."

Tears streamed down her cheeks. Something released.

> "She's been trying so hard," she said quietly. "I didn't realize how much pressure I've put on her to be perfect."

That session didn't make the pattern vanish, but it cracked it open. And that opening allowed love to pour in.

💜 Healing Affirmation

Affirmation
I am enough.
I have always been enough.
I will always be enough.

Speak it. Sing it. Write it on your mirror. Let it echo inside until it becomes your baseline belief.

Healing Practice: Reclaiming Enoughness

This ritual reconnects you to your innate worth.

1. Light a candle and sit with a photo of your younger self (or simply close your eyes and visualize).
2. Place your hands over your heart. Breathe into that image of yourself.

3. Speak aloud:

4. "You don't have to prove anything. *I love you just as you are.*"

5. Sit in silence for a few minutes. Let that truth sink in.

Do this often, especially when you feel yourself slipping into overperformance or self-doubt.

◎ *Embodiment Practice: "I Belong in My Body"*

This movement practice anchors self-worth into your physical form.

1. Stand with feet grounded and knees soft.

2. As you inhale, stretch your arms wide and say:

3. *"I take up space."*

4. As you exhale, bring your arms to hug your body and say:

5. *"I belong here."*

6. Repeat 5 times, letting the rhythm become a dance.

7. End with hands over your heart:

8. *"I am enough."*

Let your body memorize this feeling of presence, not performance.

📓 Journal Reflections

Where did I first learn I had to earn love, attention, or safety?

_____

_____

_____

_____

_____

What do I fear would happen if I believed I was already enough?

_____

_____

_____

_____

_____

In what areas of life do I still overperform to feel worthy?

_____

_____

_____

_____

What would change if I met myself with unconditional regard?

_____

_____

_____

_____

_____

A Sacred Return

You are not a project to fix or a performance to perfect.

You are a soul. So perfectly human. So exquisitely formed. So deeply worthy.

Let this be the chapter where you remember what's always been true:

You are enough.

Not someday.

Not when you hit the goal.

Not when you lose weight.

Not when you finally rest.

Not when they finally approve.

Now.

Exactly as you are.

In this breath.

In this body.

In this moment.

You are enough.

You are enough.

You are enough.

And you always have been.

Part V: Healing After Sexual Abuse

Chapter 22: Releasing the Blame that was Never Yours

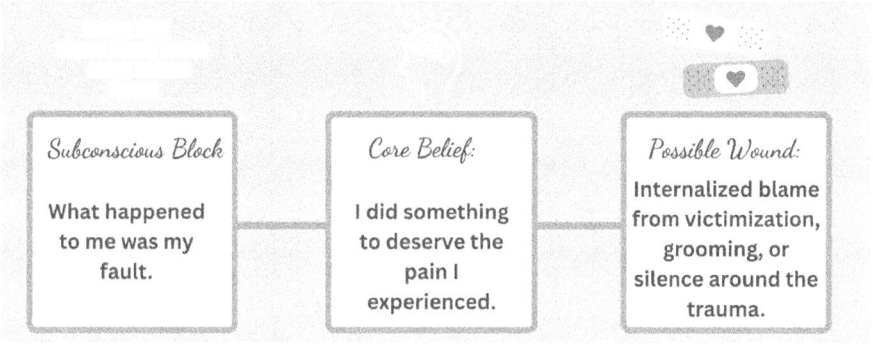

Subconscious Block	Core Belief:	Possible Wound:
What happened to me was my fault.	I did something to deserve the pain I experienced.	Internalized blame from victimization, grooming, or silence around the trauma.

When Lila began our sessions, she was calm, articulate, and deeply compassionate toward others. But not toward herself.

"Intellectually, I know it wasn't my fault," she said during an energy healing session, "but there's this voice inside that says ... *I let it happen.* If I had done something differently—dressed differently, said no louder, gotten out faster—maybe I wouldn't be carrying all this shame." She pressed her hands into her lap as her eyes welled up. "I know it sounds irrational, but part of me still thinks I caused it."

This is one of the most tender wounds to heal: *the internalized lie of blame.*

How the Blame Gets In

When children, teens, or even adults are hurt, and no one validates the pain, or worse—questions it—the psyche looks for an explanation. And often, the only one it can find is:

"It must've been me."

Especially in systems where the trauma is minimized, silenced, or spiritualized as a "lesson."

Lila had been groomed by an older man in her spiritual community, and the harm was wrapped in twisted teachings like *"You called this in for your growth"* and *"You must've had karma to clear."*

Those messages planted a belief in her that her trauma was deserved. And she carried that guilt like an invisible scar for years.

The Truth That Heals

What I told Lila, and what I offer you, is this:

There is no benefit in self-blame.
What happened to you was not your fault.
And you did not deserve it.

Not because you were naive. Not because you didn't fight hard enough. Not because you were wearing the "wrong" thing. Not because you're broken or bad.

Responsibility belongs with the one who caused harm—always.

You were never meant to carry what wasn't yours.

Lila's Turning Point

We did a reclaiming ritual where she visualized returning the shame, blame, and guilt to the one who caused the harm—not as an act of anger, but sovereignty.

She spoke aloud:

> "This shame does not belong to me.
> This guilt is not mine to carry.
> I release what was never mine."

Afterward, she said, "It felt like peeling off someone else's skin."

That's how blame leaves—not through logic, but through truth embodied.

🖤 *Healing Affirmation*

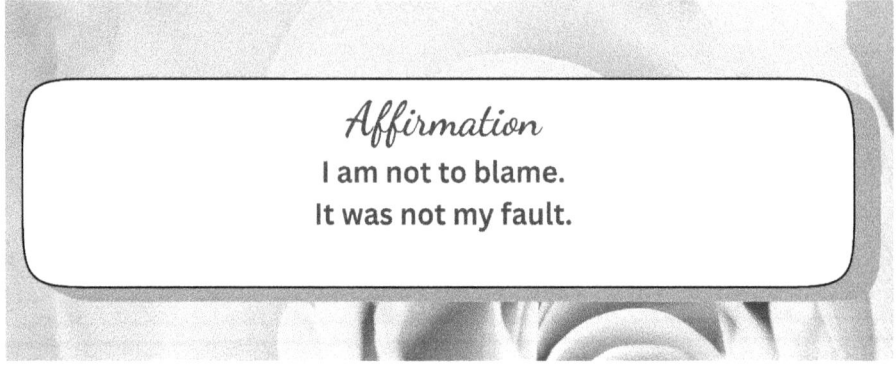

Affirmation
I am not to blame.
It was not my fault.

Speak it. Sing it. Write it on your mirror. Let it echo inside until it becomes your baseline belief.

👤 *Embodiment Practice: Shame Shedding*

1. Sit in a quiet space. Close your eyes.
2. Imagine the guilt or shame as a garment, cloak, or mist around your body.
3. With each breath, say:
4. "This is not mine."
5. "I choose to return this energy."
6. Visualize removing it—peeling, shedding, unwrapping.
7. End by placing your hands on your heart and saying:
8. *"I am innocent. I am whole. I am free."*

📓 *Journal Reflection*

What would it feel like to offer myself innocence, compassion, and release myself from blame?

Write a letter to the version of you that experienced the pain.

Remind yourself: *It wasn't your fault.*

_____

_____

_____

_____

_____

_____

_____

_____

_____

_____

Chapter 23: Reclaiming Wholeness After Shame

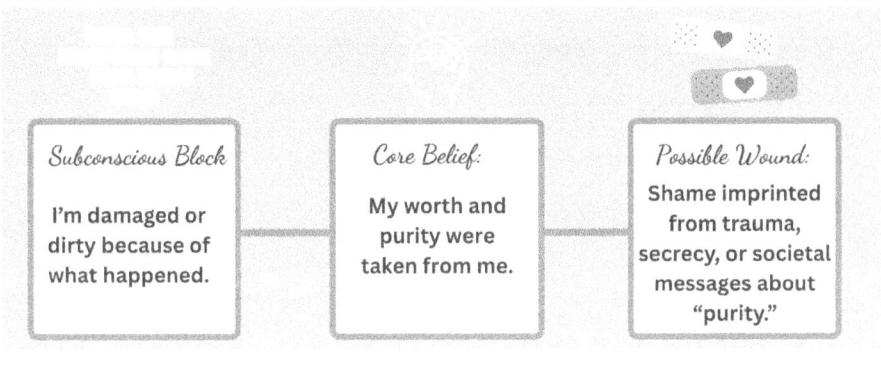

Subconscious Block	Core Belief:	Possible Wound:
I'm damaged or dirty because of what happened.	My worth and purity were taken from me.	Shame imprinted from trauma, secrecy, or societal messages about "purity."

When Tasha entered my program, she had done years of healing work, but one belief remained frozen in her body.

"I still feel like I'm stained," she told me during our first private session. "I've forgiven him. I've worked on boundaries. I've even spoken publicly about my story. But deep down, I still carry this silent belief that something in me was ruined."

She looked away when she said it, as if the words themselves carried shame.

Her trauma had happened over a decade ago. But the shame? It was still alive—not because she hadn't healed, but because her *nervous system hadn't yet been offered safety in innocence.*

Shame is Not Yours to Keep

This wound is heartbreakingly common, especially among survivors of sexual trauma, religious conditioning, or abusive relationships. Shame thrives where silence lives. And it wraps itself around our bodies, whispering lies like:

- "You're dirty."
- "You let this happen."
- "You'll never be the same."

But here's what I told Tasha and what I want to offer you with every cell of your being:

You are not damaged.

You are not dirty.

You are not ruined.

What happened to you did not remove your sacredness.

Your body is still holy. Your soul is still intact.

You are still whole.

The Origins of This Shame

Tasha was raised in a conservative household where "purity" was tied to obedience, modesty, and silence. When the abuse happened, she didn't tell anyone for years—partly because of fear, and partly because she believed she had somehow forfeited her value.

So, even as she healed cognitively, her *body still carried the imprint of contamination.*

This is how shame works. It's not just a thought. It's a *felt sense*—a heaviness, a withdrawal, a subtle contraction that says, *Don't look at me. I'm unworthy of love.*

Reclaiming the Sacred Self

In our work together, Tasha and I did a somatic reweaving process. I asked her to place one hand on her heart and the other on her womb, and repeat:

> *"I am clean. I am sacred. I am worthy of gentleness."*

At first, her body resisted. Her breath got shallow. But with practice, something softened.

She said, "I always thought I had to *forgive* to be free. But I'm realizing ... I had to *reclaim* myself first."

That moment was a homecoming.

 ## Healing Affirmation

Affirmation

**My body is sacred. I am whole, clean, and holy.
Nothing can take away my worth.**

Whisper this into the parts of you that still feel afraid to be seen.

Healing Practice: The Sacred-Self Blessing

You can do this in the mirror or with your eyes closed.

1. Place your hands over parts of your body where you've held shame—your chest, your belly, your thighs, your genitals, your heart.

2. Speak blessings aloud (use the words "I am" or "You are"—whichever speaks to you best):
   - "You are good."
   - "You are safe."
   - "You are sacred."
   - "You are mine."

3. End by wrapping your arms around yourself and saying:

4. "Nothing can take my wholeness away."

Repeat weekly or anytime the shame resurfaces.

⊚ *Embodiment Practice: The Holy Vessel Walk*

1. Light a candle and set an intention to walk as if you are the Divine in motion.

2. Walk slowly through your room or outside, with your head lifted and body open.

3. With each step, affirm:

4. *"I am holy. I am whole. I am home."*

This repatterns the subconscious into feeling reverence in the physical.

📓 Journal Reflections

Where did I learn that my value was tied to "purity"?

_____

_____

_____

_____

_____

What parts of my body still carry shame? What do they need from me now?

_____

_____

_____

_____

_____

If I saw myself as sacred, what would shift in how I move, dress, speak, or rest?

_____

_____

_____

_____

_____

What parts of me are still whole, strong, and radiant despite what I've been through?

_____

_____

_____

_____

_____

You Were Never Broken

You are not what happened to you.

You are not the silence that followed.

You are not the shame someone else placed on your shoulders.

You are the light that never went out.

The breath that kept going.

The softness that survived.

The soul that stayed intact.

Let this be the chapter where you remember:

> *You do not have to be perfect to be pure.*
> *You do not have to be untouched to be holy.*
> *You do not have to erase your story to reclaim your sacredness.*

You are clean.
You are whole.
You are still, and always, enough.

Chapter 24: Rebuilding Trust with Your Body

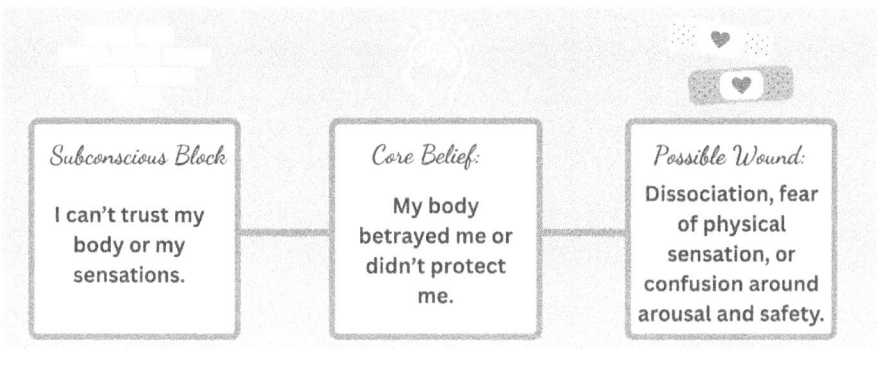

Subconscious Block	Core Belief:	Possible Wound:
I can't trust my body or my sensations.	My body betrayed me or didn't protect me.	Dissociation, fear of physical sensation, or confusion around arousal and safety.

Arielle came into our circle because, in her words, she felt "cut off" from her own skin.

"I feel like my body betrayed me," she said, "It didn't fight. It didn't protect me. And now I can't tell what's real and what's fear. Sometimes, even a kind touch or a loving gaze sends me into panic. I just … can't trust what I feel." Tears filled her eyes. "I want to come home to myself, but I don't know how."

That moment of vulnerable honesty was the doorway to healing. Because naming the rupture is the first step toward reweaving trust with the body.

The Truth About Betrayal and Survival

What I shared with Arielle and what I'll share with you is this:

Your body did not betray you.
It protected you in the only way it knew how.

When trauma happens, especially trauma involving the body, your nervous system reacts in ways you don't consciously control. You may freeze, dissociate, go numb, or shut down. These are not failures—they are *instinctive, intelligent survival responses.*

But when the danger passes and the pattern remains, you can begin to mistrust the very system that helped you survive.

That's the cruel paradox: the body saved us, but afterward, it feels like the enemy.

How Trauma Breaks Trust with the Body

Arielle had experienced childhood abuse, and later, an emotionally coercive relationship that blurred her sense of boundaries and bodily autonomy.

Her relationship with sensation was deeply conflicted. She either felt *nothing* or *too much*. Touch was either dissociative or overwhelming. Pleasure, arousal, even hunger confused her.

She had internalized the belief that her sensations were unreliable. Unsafe.

And yet, her longing was clear: *to come home to her body—not in fear, but in safety.*

The Path of Reconnection

Healing in this area is not about "feeling good" right away—it's about *feeling safe enough to feel at all.*

With Arielle, we started small. Micro-moments of safety. We used the language of attunement, not force. The goal wasn't to fix the body, but to *befriend* it again.

We used:

- Grounding
- Energy healing
- Energetic boundary practices
- Safe pleasure practices
- Nervous system regulation
- Compassionate presence

Over time, she began to notice when she was *in* her body. And, more importantly, when she could stay.

Arielle's Turning Point

One day, after practicing a simple breath-and-touch ritual for several weeks, she texted me:

"I sat in the salt bath last night and felt my whole body. Not fear. Not judgment. Just sensation. And I didn't run. I stayed. I think I'm starting to trust her again."

Her body had gone from battlefield to sanctuary.

That's what's possible.

 Healing Affirmation

Affirmation

My body is my ally.
I am learning to feel safe, connected, and at home again.

Speak this slowly, perhaps placing one hand over your heart and the other over your lower belly. Let your nervous system register it as truth.

Healing Practice: The 5-Minute Sensation Scan

Use this gentle practice to build trust with sensation, without judgment or pressure.

1. Find a quiet space and sit or lie down.
2. Close your eyes and slowly scan from your toes to your head.
3. Ask, "What am I sensing here?"
4. Warmth? Coolness? Tingling? Numbness? Pressure?
5. If you feel nothing, that's okay. Say aloud:
6. "It's safe to feel nothing right now."
7. If you feel too much, open your eyes, place your hand on your heart, and say:
8. *"I am here. I am safe."*

Repeat this practice daily. Think of it as your body's way of learning to trust your attention again.

⊚ *Embodiment Practice: Safe Touch Ritual*

1. Choose an area of your body that feels neutral or calm (e.g., forearms, thighs, scalp).
2. With gentle, intentional contact, massage that area for 1-3 minutes.
3. Repeat a loving phrase as you touch, such as:
4. *"I am safe now."*
5. "I am with you."
6. "This touch is mine."

Use soothing music or silence. Always go slow. The goal is *connection,* and it's also ok if you feel pleasure or stimulation.

📓 *Journal Reflections*

When did I first learn to mistrust my body's signals?

_____

_____

_____

_____

_____

What sensations feel safe to me right now? What still feels scary?

_____

_____

_____

_____

_____

What might it feel like to treat my body as a wise friend rather than a faulty machine?

_____

_____

_____

_____

_____

What are three small ways I could begin rebuilding trust with my body this week?

_____

_____

_____

_____

_____

You Can Return

You do not have to force a reunion with your body.

You are not late. You are not broken.

You are not failing if it still feels hard to feel.

The body is patient. She waits for you—not with shame, but with *longing*.

Let this be the chapter where you begin again—not with pressure, but with presence.

You are not lost.

You are returning.

And your body is ready to welcome you home.

Chapter 25: Reclaiming Safe Sensuality and Radiance

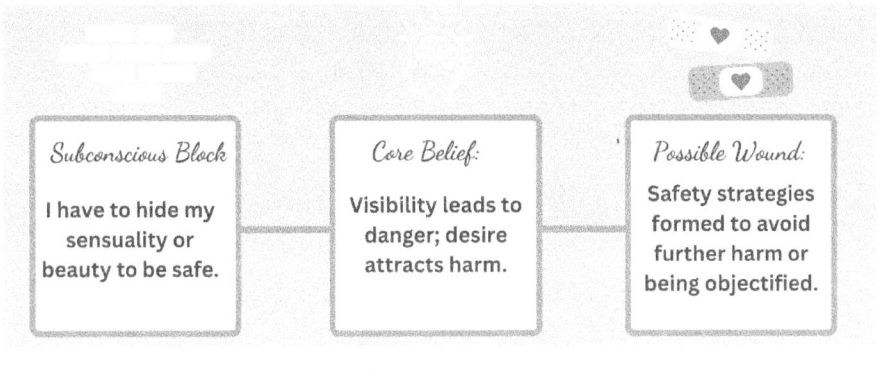

Subconscious Block	Core Belief:	Possible Wound:
I have to hide my sensuality or beauty to be safe.	Visibility leads to danger; desire attracts harm.	Safety strategies formed to avoid further harm or being objectified.

Elena had magnetic energy, even on Zoom.

She radiated wisdom, creativity, and warmth. But when the topic turned to reclaiming body confidence, something shifted. She crossed her arms. Her eyes dropped.

"I've worked hard to feel safe in my body again," she said. "But any time I dress up, or someone compliments me ... I shrink. I shut it down. It's like my system doesn't want to be noticed." She took a breath and added, "I used to love being seen. But now, it feels like being seen = being unsafe."

Elena wasn't exaggerating. She was remembering. And her body still carried that memory like a protective veil.

When Visibility Becomes a Threat

Elena had experienced sexual trauma in college. Afterward, she unconsciously began dimming her light. She wore looser clothing. Avoided makeup. Withdrew from dating. She didn't just stop flirting—she stopped *glowing*.

"I felt like if I was attractive, I was inviting harm," she said. "So I stopped being attractive, even to myself."

For many survivors, sensuality becomes conflated with danger. Beauty becomes a liability. Radiance feels risky.

This is not vanity—it's a *nervous system adaptation*. It's what we do to protect ourselves when our magnetism has once been weaponized or misinterpreted.

But you were never meant to live in hiding. You were born to shine.

Healing the Split Between Beauty and Safety

What I shared with Elena and what I offer you is this:

> *It is safe to be seen.*
> *It is safe to radiate.*
> *It is safe to enjoy your own beauty and sensuality—on your terms.*

Your sensuality is not a threat. It is not a promise. It is not an invitation for exploitation. It is *an extension of your spirit.*

It is your birthright to feel turned on by life, by movement, by texture, by color, by your own reflection.

And that radiance? It belongs to *you.*

Elena's Turning Point

We began with gentle permission—no pressure to "reclaim" anything. Just curiosity.

In one session, I invited her to spend time each day doing something sensual—not sexual—just something that awakened pleasure in her body *for her.* A silk robe. Scented lotion. Music that moved her hips.

A few weeks later, she came to our call smiling.

"I wore lipstick and danced in my living room," she said. "I didn't post about it. I didn't do it for anyone else. It was *mine.* And, for the first time in years, I felt like I was safe to be beautiful again."

That's what reclaiming looks like: sovereignty, not show.

♥ *Healing Affirmation*

Affirmation
**My sensuality is mine to own and express.
I am safe, sovereign, and radiant.**

Speak this while placing one hand on your heart and one on your lower belly. Let the words ripple through your body like a blessing.

Healing Practice: The Radiance Mirror Ritual

1. Set the tone—light a candle or play music that makes you feel grounded.
2. Stand in front of a mirror and look into your own eyes.
3. Say:
4. "I see myself. I choose to see ME. I choose to LOVE me."
5. Then slowly observe your face, your shape, your energy.
6. Choose one feature to compliment out loud.
7. End with:

8. *"It is safe to glow. I belong to myself."*

This ritual helps desensitize fear and build a new association between visibility and safety.

⊚ *Embodiment Practice: Safe Sensuality Movement*

1. Choose a song that evokes warmth or joy, not intensity.
2. Let your body move with curiosity, not performance.
3. Focus on how the fabric of your clothes feels, how your skin responds to rhythm.
4. Say aloud:
5. *"This sensation is for me. This pleasure is mine."*

This helps separate sensuality from performative or people-pleasing patterns and roots it in embodied autonomy.

Journal Reflections

When did I first start to believe that being visible or beautiful was unsafe?

_____

_____

_____

_____

_____

What beliefs do I carry about sensuality and danger?

_____

_____

_____

_____

_____

What expressions of beauty or radiance have I hidden to stay "safe?"

_____

_____

_____

_____

_____

- What parts of my feminine or sensual self am I ready to reclaim?

_____

_____

_____

_____

Your Light is Not a Threat

You don't have to dim your shine to protect yourself.

You don't have to be invisible to be safe.

You don't have to disconnect from beauty or sensuality to be spiritual, respected, or in control.

Let this be the chapter where you reclaim:

- *Your hips.*
- *Your womb.*
- *Your heart.*
- *Your glow.*
- *Your pleasure.*
- *Your flirtation with life.*

Let this be the moment you decide:

> "I will not hide. I will not shrink. I will not fear my own light."

Your sensuality is not a risk.

It is your *sovereign glow.*

Chapter 26: Believing in Your Capacity to Heal

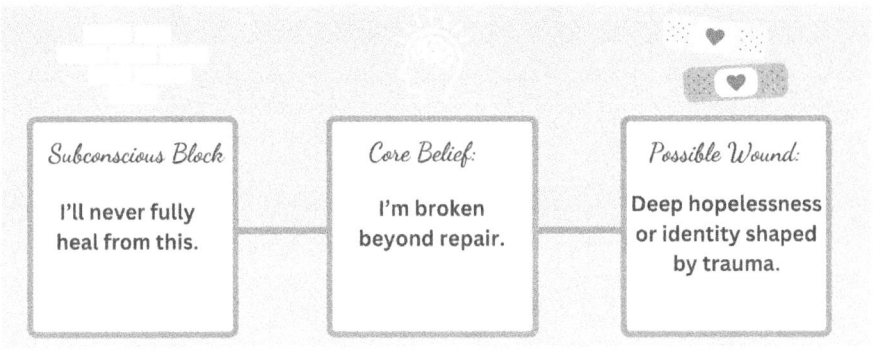

Subconscious Block	Core Belief:	Possible Wound:
I'll never fully heal from this.	I'm broken beyond repair.	Deep hopelessness or identity shaped by trauma.

Carmen came into my practice with decades of spiritual work, therapy, and somatic healing under her belt.

"I'm tired," she said softly. "I've made so much progress … but sometimes it still hurts. And I wonder: will it ever *really* go away?" Her eyes welled with tears. "Maybe this is just who I am now—a person who's been through something and will always carry the ache."

There was no drama in her voice. No self-pity. Just quiet exhaustion. The kind that creeps in after years of trying, crying, rising, and repeating.

And the fear behind it: *Maybe this wound is too deep to ever truly heal.*

When the Wound Becomes the Identity

For many survivors, trauma becomes fused with identity—not because we want it to, but because it's how we've learned to explain the world. To make sense of pain. To stay safe.

Carmen had done a tremendous amount of healing, but she still measured her growth against whether or not the pain ever came back.

And when it did—through a memory, a body flashback, or an unexpected trigger—she would spiral into discouragement.

"Shouldn't I be past this by now?" she'd ask.

I looked at her gently and said:

> *Healing isn't a straight line. It's a sacred spiral.*
> *You return to the wound not because you've failed,*
> *but because each time, you meet it with more of*
> *your self.*

You are Not Broken

This chapter is not here to promise a pain-free life.

It's here to remind you:

> *You can live a beautiful life, even with what you've*
> *been through.*
> *You can experience joy, pleasure, and purpose,*
> *even if grief still visits.*

You can be whole, even if healing is still happening.

Carmen had been waiting for a day when the pain would vanish completely.

But what we uncovered together was something more powerful:

You don't have to wait for the wound to disappear before you declare yourself whole.

Carmen's Turning Point

In one session, I invited her to speak directly to the part of her that felt hopeless.

She placed her hands over her heart and belly and whispered:

"I know you're tired. I'm here. I've got us now."

Something softened in her body.

She cried—not because she was broken, but because she realized she *never had been.*

She was carrying a wound, but she was also carrying wisdom, strength, and a powerful will to live in alignment with who she truly is.

💜 Healing Affirmation

> ### Affirmation
>
> **Healing is my birthright.**
> **I am resilient, and my spirit is stronger than what happened.**

Speak this each morning, especially on the days you feel like giving up. Let it root you in remembrance.

Healing Practice: Your Resilience Timeline

This practice helps shift your focus from "what still hurts" to "how far I've come."

1. On a blank page, draw a horizontal timeline.
2. Mark key moments of your healing:
   - When you left the harmful relationship
   - When you told your story
   - When you started therapy
   - When you felt joy again
3. Under each moment, write:
4. "I survived this. I grew from this. *I'm proud of myself.*"
5. Add new milestones as you go. Let this timeline be a living document of your sacred resilience.

◎ *Embodiment Practice: Wholeness Meditation*

1. Sit comfortably. Close your eyes.
2. Visualize yourself surrounded by a golden light.
3. With each inhale, breathe in the words:
4. "I am whole."
5. With each exhale:
6. *"I am healing."*
7. Let your body feel held by the earth, by love, by Source.
8. End by placing your hands on your heart and whispering:
9. "I am not what happened. I am who I've become."

📓 Journal Reflections

What story have I been telling myself about my healing journey?

_____

_____

_____

_____

_____

What parts of me have grown stronger through this process?

_____

_____

_____

_____

_____

When was the last time I felt proud of my progress?

_____

_____

_____

_____

_____

What does wholeness mean to me, beyond perfection?

_____

_____

_____

_____

_____

Healing is Not a Destination

You do not need to wait for perfect healing to begin living.

You are not behind.

You are not broken.

You are not defined by your past—you are deepened by it.

Let this be the chapter where you stop measuring healing by the absence of pain and start measuring it by the presence of love, breath, connection, and joy.

You are healing.

You are here.

You are holy.

And your life is still unfolding with beauty, courage, and power.

Tiffany Cano

Part VI: Integration and Embodiment

27: Sacred Self-Care and Soulful Rituals

28: The Journey Home

Chapter 27: Sacred Self-Care and Soulful Rituals

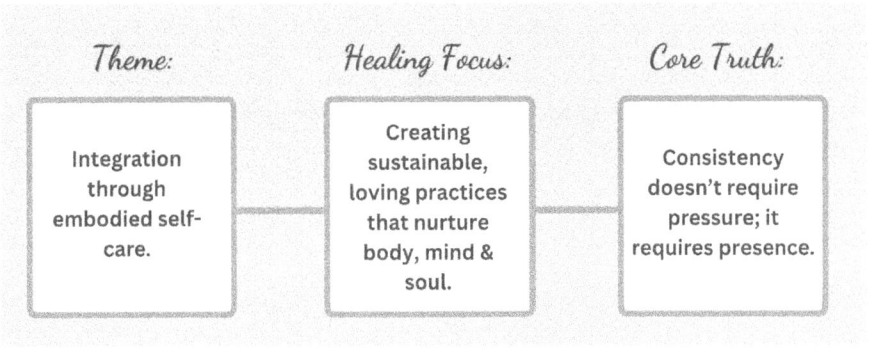

Theme:	Healing Focus:	Core Truth:
Integration through embodied self-care.	Creating sustainable, loving practices that nurture body, mind & soul.	Consistency doesn't require pressure; it requires presence.

By the time Jess reached the end of our program together, she had cleared dozens of beliefs that once weighed her down.

"I feel lighter," she said, "but I don't want to lose this momentum. I don't want this healing to be a moment—I want it to become a lifestyle."

I smiled. Because this is the crossroads that most people arrive at when their inner work starts to stick. It's the transition from breakthrough to embodiment. From insight to integration.

And that's exactly what this chapter is about.

What Integration Really Means

Healing isn't a finish line—it's a *rhythm*. A relationship. A gentle return to self over and over again.

Integration doesn't ask you to be perfect.

It asks:

- Can you check in with yourself each day?
- Can you nurture the parts of you that are still learning to feel safe in love?
- Can you make space for softness without waiting to deserve it?

Self-care, when it's sacred, is not a luxury—it's *devotion*.

Daily Sacred Practices: Grounding into You

These rituals are not "to-do list" tasks. They are invitations to come home to your body.

Try any of these as daily check-ins:

☀ Morning Ritual Ideas

- 5-Minute Body Check-In
  - Place your hands over your belly and heart. Ask, *"What do you need today?"*
- Affirmation Mirror Work
  - Look at your reflection and say:

- ○ *"Good morning, beloved. We are enough today."*
- Loving Movement
  - ○ Gentle stretches, dancing, or walking—movement that says *thank you*, not *fix yourself*.

🌙 Evening Ritual Ideas

- Compassionate Closure Journal
  - ○ Write:
    - ■ "One thing I'm proud of today …"
    - ■ "One thing I release with love …"
    - ■ "One way I'll care for myself tomorrow …"
- Body Gratitude Scan
  - ○ Lie in bed and silently thank each part of your body, head to toe.
- Boundaries Reset
  - ○ Say aloud:
  - ○ "I *release* any energy that's not mine. I return to my center."

Weekly Rituals: Creating Sacred Structure

Each week, choose 2-3 rituals to anchor your integration.

- Sunday Soul Soak
  - ○ Light candles, take a bath with oils or salts, and set intentions for the week.

- Clothing Ceremony
  - Pick an outfit that makes your body feel honored. Dress slowly, with reverence. Speak kindness into the mirror.
- Joy Reclamation Hour
  - Do something playful, artistic, or sensual, just because. Let joy be your birthright.
- Body Love Letter
  - Write a note to your body once a week.
    - *Thank you for carrying me."*
    - *"I'm learning to trust you."*
    - *"I see your strength and your softness."*

 *Habit Tracker Template*

Not to control—but to *connect*.

At the end of the week, reflect:

Habit Tracker

WEEK OF _____

HABIT	MON	TUE	WED	THU	FRI	SAT	SUN
_____	○	○	○	○	○	○	○
_____	○	○	○	○	○	○	○
_____	○	○	○	○	○	○	○
_____	○	○	○	○	○	○	○
_____	○	○	○	○	○	○	○
_____	○	○	○	○	○	○	○
_____	○	○	○	○	○	○	○
_____	○	○	○	○	○	○	○
_____	○	○	○	○	○	○	○
_____	○	○	○	○	○	○	○
_____	○	○	○	○	○	○	○
_____	○	○	○	○	○	○	○
_____	○	○	○	○	○	○	○
_____	○	○	○	○	○	○	○
_____	○	○	○	○	○	○	○
_____	○	○	○	○	○	○	○
_____	○	○	○	○	○	○	○
_____	○	○	○	○	○	○	○

- Which rituals nourished me most?
- Where did I abandon or avoid myself?
- How can I lovingly recommit?

Rebuilding Trust with Time

If you find yourself missing rituals, forgetting intentions, or falling back into old patterns, pause and remember:

You're not failing. You're recalibrating.

Your healing is not measured in checkmarks. It's measured in your return.

And you are *always allowed* to return.

Journal Reflections for Integration

What does self-care look like when it's not about control but about connection?

_____

_____

_____

_____

_____

Which rituals make me feel most anchored in love and presence?

_____

_____

_____

_____

_____

Where do I still abandon myself, and how can I offer grace instead?

_____

_____

_____

_____

_____

What rhythms or routines help me feel safe, seen, and sacred?

_____

_____

_____

_____

_____

Integration

Affirmation for Integration

I choose sacred consistency.
I honor myself with love, not pressure.
My body is my home & I am devoted to caring for her.

Let this be your north star when the world gets noisy.

A Blessing

If you've made it here—if you've traveled through the stories, the shadows, the softness—know this:

You are not just healing for yourself.

You are healing generations.

You are reclaiming joy, belonging, and body sovereignty.

You are becoming your own sanctuary.

And this—this sacred tending of your inner world—is not the end.

It's your beginning.

Let every ritual be a love note.

Let every breath be a homecoming.

Let your body be the altar, and your care be the prayer.

You belong here.

You always have.

 Chapter 28: The Journey Home

As you close the final pages of *Sacred Body, Sacred Soul*, I want you to pause for a moment and feel just how much you've done.

You've walked through layers of old shame and self-judgment.

You've breathed life back into places inside you that were once abandoned.

You've listened, softened, dared to feel, and dared to hope.

You have said "yes" to yourself, again and again.

That is no small thing.

That is a sacred act of courage.

If no one has told you yet today ...

I am so proud of you.

You should be proud of yourself, too.

Healing is not about arriving at perfection.

Healing is about becoming more *intimately, honestly, and tenderly* connected to your sacred self.

And look, you are here.

❋ Welcoming Your Healing

Throughout this journey, you have planted seeds inside you.

Some seeds may already be blossoming—new thoughts, new boundaries, new tenderness toward yourself.

Other seeds may still be buried beneath the soil of your subconscious, quietly gathering strength.

Both are beautiful.

Both are sacred.

Healing isn't linear.

It isn't something you finish.

It's something you *live.*

Every moment you choose self-compassion over self-criticism,

every breath you take to ground yourself when old fear arises,

every loving thought you offer your body,

you are integrating your healing.

You are weaving sacredness into the very fabric of your life.

Notice and Celebrate

I invite you to color in your level of satisfaction.

Notice the positive, empowering shifts of your life after going through the whole book.

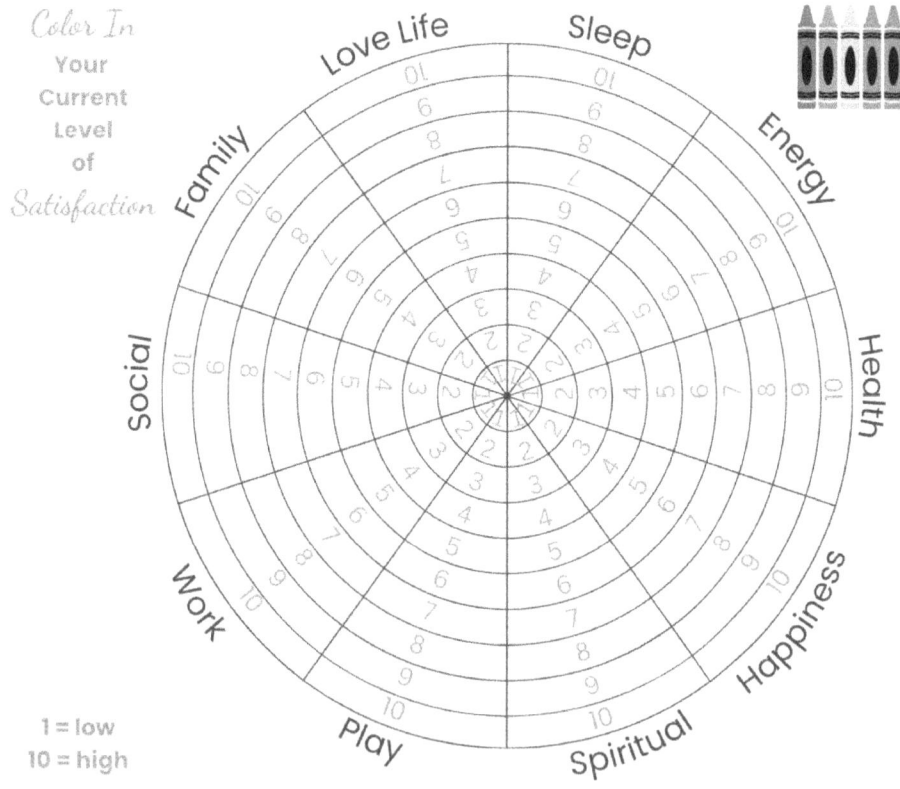

Color In
Your
Current
Level
of
Satisfaction

1 = low
10 = high

🌿 Embodying Your Sacredness

You didn't read this book to learn *about* healing.

You *lived* it. You *felt* it. You *became* it.

And now, the invitation is to continue embodying your sacredness in your daily life.

Not by force.

Not by pressure.

But by *allowing*.

Here are some gentle ways to keep integrating the healing you've unlocked:

- **Morning Intentions:** Before your day begins, whisper an affirmation:
- *"I choose to walk in my sacredness today."*
- *"I honor my body, my soul, and my spirit."*
- **Micro-Moments of Self-Compassion:** When you catch an old thought pattern sneaking in, pause.
- Smile softly.
- *Offer yourself* kindness instead of criticism.
- Remember: You are building new, sacred pathways inside your mind and body.
- **Sacred Sensual Rituals:** Let your senses *awaken to pleasure* again—touch, taste, sound, scent, beauty.
- Sensuality, in its purest form, is a homecoming to your aliveness.

- **Boundary Blessings:** *Boundaries* are not walls; they are sacred doors that honor your wholeness.
- Protect your energy with love, not fear.
- **Ceremonies of Celebration:** Celebrate your milestones, no matter how small.
- Acknowledging your growth *anchors it into your body.*

You are not starting from scratch.

You are building upon the sacred foundation you've remembered here.

As an additional way to celebrate, consider completing the Self-Assessment to show your improvement.

Sacred Body, Sacred Soul
Self-Reflection Scale
Please Rate Yourself (1–10 scale)

.... I feel safe and at home in my body.

.... I treat myself with compassion and kindness.

.... I feel comfortable being seen and taking up space.

.... I trust my body's wisdom and signals.

.... I feel worthy of love regardless of how I look.

.... I have healthy boundaries with others and myself.

.... I feel connected to my sacred feminine/masculine essence.

.... I honor my emotions without judgment.

.... I feel confident in my sensuality or softness.

.... I believe I am already whole.

You are the Healing

One of the most beautiful truths I've seen time and again in my work is this:

> Healing isn't something that happens *to* you.
>
> Healing is something that happens *through* you.
>
> You are wholeness awakening itself.
>
> *You are love,* remembering its form.

You are already everything you've been seeking.

This book didn't *give* you that.

It simply helped you *remember*.

🌿 *When You Feel Yourself Forgetting*

And yes, because you are beautifully human, you might sometimes forget again.

You might slip back into old patterns.

You might feel moments of fear, shame, or disconnection.

That's okay.

It's part of the spiral of healing.

Each time you return to yourself with love, you deepen your roots.

When you notice yourself forgetting, whisper:

"I choose to remember now."

Come back to your breath.

Come back to your body.

Come back to your sacredness.

You are never starting over.

You are simply coming home, again and again, more tenderly each time.

🌸 *If You Need Support, You're Not Alone*

While you've made incredible strides through this book, you don't have to walk the next part of your journey alone.

Sometimes, deeper healing calls for sacred witnessing.

For loving space-holding.

For intuitive guidance, gentle clearing, and soul-deep integration.

If you feel your heart calling for additional support, I would be honored to continue walking beside you. 🌿

You are invited to schedule a private healing consultation with me at:

👉 www.CallwithTiffany.com

Whether you are ready to deepen your embodiment, clear old layers that still linger, or simply be held in a sacred container of love and possibility, there is a path waiting for you.

One where you are *honored.*

One where you are *empowered.*

One where you are deeply, tenderly supported in becoming the fullest expression of your *sacred body* and *sacred soul.*

🌿 Parting Blessing

Before you close this book, I invite you to place one hand over your heart and one hand over your lower belly.

Feel your body breathe.

Feel your heart open.

Feel the miracle of your existence.

And say softly to yourself:

> *"I honor my sacred body.*
>
> *I honor my sacred soul.*
>
> *I welcome my healing.*
>
> *I trust my journey.*
>
> *I am home."*

May your days ahead be filled with tenderness.

May your body feel like a temple you love to live in.

May your soul dance freely in the sacredness of your life.

Thank you for trusting me to walk this part of your journey with you.

It has been a deep honor, and it always will be.

Your healing has already begun.

Your sacred body and sacred soul are already shining.

And the world is blessed because you are here.

Love, love, love ...

Additional Resources:

The healing work continues beyond these pages.

Highly Perceptive People Academy

Whether through one-on-one sessions, online programs, healing retreats, or our global Highly Perceptive People Academy community, you are welcome.

https://HighlyPerceptivePeopleAcademy.com

Sacred Body, Sacred Soul Bonus Gifts

Want even more support and free gifts to accompany this book?

www.SacredBodySacredSoul.com has bonus gifts to accompany you on your healing journey.

You are worthy of deep, embodied healing.

And I am honored to hold space for you.

Tiffany's Cell Phone App:

www.TiffanysApp.com

Receive a free Mantra Song as a free bonus when you go to

www.SacredBodySacredSoul.com.

The accompanied workbook is also available for purchase.

Tiffany's Upcoming Movie Documentaries that are coming out on major streaming services:

> **Pillars of Power: Discovering the Hidden Secrets Behind Achieving Greatness** (Releasing Fall 2025)

Frequency of Miracles: Discover the Universes Secret to Success (Releasing Fall 2025)

Rise of the Lioness: The Power of Feminine Leadership (Releasing 2026)

Upcoming Books:

Sacred Money, Sacred Soul

Sacred Health, Sacred Soul

Sacred You, Sacred Soul

Tiffany Cano

References:

🔬 Scientific Research Validating Trauma and Emotional Transmission Through DNA (Epigenetics)

---

1. Holocaust Survivors and Their Offspring

Dr. Rachel Yehuda's groundbreaking research found that Holocaust survivors' children exhibited epigenetic changes in the FKBP5 gene, which plays a role in stress regulation. These changes were not just psychological but **biologically measurable**, suggesting trauma can be inherited.

- 🔗 [Scientific American Article: How Parents' Trauma Leaves Biological Traces in Children](#)

Reference:

Yehuda, R., Daskalakis, N.P., Bierer, L.M., Bader, H.N., Klengel, T., Holsboer, F., & Binder, E.B. (2016). Holocaust Exposure Induced Intergenerational Effects on FKBP5 Methylation. *Biological Psychiatry*, 80(5), 372-380. DOI: 10.1016/j.biopsych.2015.08.005

---

2. Syrian Refugees and War-Related Trauma

Recent studies on Syrian refugees revealed that traumatic war experiences led to DNA methylation changes, which could impact not only the survivors but also future generations' physical and emotional health.

- 🔗 Nature Study: Multigenerational Epigenetic Effects of War Trauma

Reference:

Ouellet-Morin, I., et al. (2025). Multigenerational Epigenetic Effects of War Trauma: Evidence from Syrian Refugees. *Scientific Reports (Nature)*. DOI: 10.1038/s41598-025-89818-z

---

3. Animal Studies Showing Trauma Passed Through Sperm

Mouse studies demonstrate that traumatic experiences can alter DNA methylation patterns in sperm, and these alterations can affect the offspring's brain development and behavior, showing direct transmission of trauma-related responses across generations.

- 🔗 Science.org Article: Parents' Emotional Trauma May Change Children's Biology

Reference:

Gapp, K., et al. (2014). Implication of sperm RNAs in transgenerational inheritance of the effects of early trauma in mice. *Nature Neuroscience*, 17(5), 667-669. DOI: 10.1038/nn.3695

---

4. Intergenerational Transmission of Trauma: Scientific Review

This review in *Frontiers in Psychiatry* provides a broader look at how trauma-induced epigenetic changes are passed down and how they could predispose descendants to mental health challenges.

- 🔗 <u>Frontiers in Psychiatry: Review on Trauma Transmission via Epigenetics</u>

Reference:

Yehuda, R., Lehrner, A., & Bierer, L.M. (2018). The HPA Axis and the Epigenetic Transmission of Stress Responses Through DNA Methylation. *Frontiers in Psychiatry*, 9, 72. DOI: 10.3389/fpsyt.2018.00072

🧬 Summary of Epigenetic Mechanisms Involved

- **DNA Methylation:** Trauma changes how genes related to stress responses are "turned on" or "turned off."
- **Histone Modification:** Trauma can affect how tightly DNA is packaged, influencing gene expression.

- **Non-Coding RNAs:** These molecules help regulate which genes are expressed, influenced by environmental and emotional factors.

Journal Page

Journal Page

Journal Page

www.ingramcontent.com/pod-product-compliance
Lightning Source LLC
Chambersburg PA
CBHW051609120626
46551CB00014B/1731